THE WISE WOMAN

Judy Hall has been running workshops in healing, complementary medicine and astrology for many years. Drawing both from personal experience and from her training as a counsellor, she runs a successful private practice and regular workshops with her partner, Dr Robert Jacobs, where she helps many women through their midlife transition.

Dr Robert Jacobs is a practising medical doctor and acupuncturist who has combined conventional medical training with a study of eastern philosophies and systems of healing.

Also by Judy Hall

THE KARMIC JOURNEY: THE BIRTHCHART,
KARMA AND REINCARNATION

The
Wise Woman

A NATURAL APPROACH
TO THE MENOPAUSE

JUDY HALL

WITH
DR ROBERT JACOBS MRCS LRCP

ELEMENT
Shaftesbury, Dorset ● Rockport, Massachusetts

Published in Great Britain in 1992 by
Element Books Limited
Longmead, Shaftesbury, Dorset

Published in the USA in 1992 by
Element, Inc
42 Broadway, Rockport, MA 01966

Cover design by Max Fairbrother
Designed by Roger Lightfoot
Phototypeset by Intype Ltd, London
Printed and bound in Great Britain
by Dotesios Ltd, Trowbridge, Wiltshire

British Library Cataloguing in Publication Data
A catalogue record for this book
is available from the British Library

Library of Congress Data available

ISBN 1-85230-344-1

Contents

For Liz
guide, mentor, friend
and a very Wise Woman indeed
who taught me that

Change is not made without inconvenience,
even from worse to better.

Richard Hooker

Acknowledgements

We would especially like to thank Sarah Litvinoff, and our editor Julia McCutchen of Element Books, for all their help, encouragement and support during the writing of this book.

As several of your stories are told in the book, we have not mentioned friends by name, but you will know who you are and you have our loving thanks for all your wisdom – and patience when it seemed that the menopause was the only topic of conversation!

In addition, to all the women who have contributed their stories both to the book and in workshops, grateful thanks for being so open. We learned so much from you.

To Judy's daughter, Jeni Campbell, go special thanks for the beautiful illustrations she so lovingly created. It took a special intuition and much talent to manifest Judy's inner vision.

Robert Jacobs wishes to thank all those who have taught him medicine over the years, in particular those whose ideas have been an inspiration for this book including Dr June Burger, Dr Julian Kenyon, and Mr Michael McIntyre.

Acknowledgements are due to the following for kindly giving permission to quote in this book:

Julie Felix for the words to 'Woman', copyright © Julie Felix 1990.

HarperCollins Publishers for the extracts from *Your Menopause* by Myra Hunter (Pandora Press), *Goddesses in Everywoman* by Jean Shinoda Bolen, *The Great Cosmic Mother* by Monica Sjoo and Barbara Mor, and *Women of a Certain Age*, by Lillian B. Rubin.

Lillian B. Rubin for *Women of a Certain Age*.

The Return of the Goddess by Edward C. Whitmont. Copyright © 1982 by Edward C. Whitmont. Reprinted by permission of The Crossroad Publishing Co. and Penguin Books Ltd.

Extract from Novak's *Gynecology* by kind permission of Dr Howard W. Jones III MD and © Williams & Wilkins Co, Baltimore.

Honora Lee Wolfe and Blue Poppy Press for *Second Spring*.

The Independent on Sunday and Maureen Freely for extract from 'We shall not be moved'.

Quartet Books Limited for *The Mirror Within* by Anne Dickson.

Prentice-Hall Inc for *Death, The Final Stage of Growth* by Elisabeth Kubler-Ross.

Llewellyn Worldwide Inc for *Chiron* by Barbara Hand Clow.

Yes International Publishers for *The Spiral Path* by Theresa King O'Brien and Chandra Patel.

Journal of Chinese Medicine for extract from the article on 'Menopause' by Jane Lyttleton, Issue 39.

Note: Every effort has been made to trace the copyright holders of works quoted from in this book, but in some cases this has not proved possible. The authors and publishers therefore wish to thank the authors or copyright holders of any material which is included without acknowledgement above.

INTRODUCTION

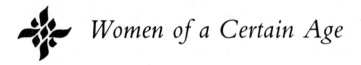 *Women of a Certain Age*

The menopause is one of life's milestones

Myra Hunter[1]

THE MENOPAUSE EXPERIENCE

The menopause is one of the major periods of change for women, yet it is rarely understood and frequently causes considerable inner pain and outer discomfort. The subject of innumerable fallacies and misconceptions, it is still a taboo topic for many women even though it has been estimated that, by the mid-1990s in Britain alone, approximately seven million women will be entering, experiencing, or moving out of the menopause.[2]

One of the major western fallacies over the last hundred years or so was that menopausal women were irrational figures: subject to hysterical moods which turned them into screaming harpies one minute and kleptomaniacs the next. In the western tradition, menopausal women have been regarded as 'has-beens' who have reached the end of their useful life in society. However, with the lengthening of life expectancy and following the impetus of the women's movement, a 'new' woman is emerging: one who is eager to take up the challenge offered by the change of life, and who recognizes that she has considerable wisdom and experience to offer society. Unfortunately, however, within society as a whole the taboo of menopause still has to be removed, together with the invisibility thrust on many post-menopausal women.

Women themselves may be partly to blame for this 'invisibility'. When Jungian analyst Ann Mankowitz researched the menopause in the early 1980s, she found a curious ambivalence in women and a conflict between 'the fear of knowing and the need to know',[3] together with a puzzling lack of positive literature on the subject. This ambivalence has continued into the 1990s despite, or maybe because of, the proliferation of 'self help' books and the increasing prescription of hormones by doctors to deal with the symptoms of The Change. Due to the negative stereotypes which still exist, women are reluctant to admit that they have reached 'that certain age', and the taboos surrounding the menopause are still firmly in place, particularly as the post-menopausal woman has no socially defined role to play in society.

However, if the menopause can be seen as a natural staging post on the journey of life, then it can become a time of positive change and infinite possibilities. As author Barbara Walker points out, in ancient societies post-menopausal women were thought to be the most effective callers down of curses as 'their "wise blood" was retained in their bodies, giving them a numinous power to make their words come true.'[4] This book seeks to use the potency of 'wise blood' to transform what may have been experienced as a curse into a blessing!

This book arose out of my own shock and horror at finding myself confronting a variety of bizarre symptoms which were tenuously linked together by the theme of 'It's your age' and the tentative diagnosis of pre-menopausal hormonal changes. Having had an adverse reaction to just one week of hormone treatment (undertaken out of urgent need and desperation), and having been involved with complementary medicine and psychological counselling for many years, I decided to seek a different solution to the problem. I am fortunate in sharing my life with a doctor who utilizes a combination of therapies and who has written the chapters on conventional and alternative medical approaches to the menopause. The complementary treatment revolutionized my energy and alleviated my symptoms. But, from discussion with women who were undergoing many facets of the same experience, I realized that the changes now facing me arose not only on the physical level but were also mental, emotional and spiritual, and therefore required a truly holistic approach.

Each woman's experience of the menopause is uniquely individual but there are common factors, and knowledge about these can avoid the feeling of isolation which often accompanies the menopause. Whilst menopause is not a disease, nevertheless the physiological changes can give rise to a variety of 'symptoms'. (The use of the word 'symptom' does not however imply that the menopause is a medical disorder.) Many women never experience physical symptoms or discomfort during this phase of life; others can be totally devastated by them. But almost all women are affected to a greater or lesser degree emotionally and mentally, and may face a crisis of identity or purpose which shakes them to their very foundations. Whilst you will most certainly not encounter all the problems covered here, you may well find several that are relevant to your own particular circumstances and experience. The problems are covered in detail so that every woman can identify her own particular response to the hormonal changes and life challenges offered by the menopause. The book, however, also brings the message that these difficulties can be overcome and that there is life after menopause after all.

From my experience in running workshops and within my counselling practice, it is my belief that menopausal women need a space to mourn lost fertility and to heal psychic pain. They need an opportunity to discover, and reframe, the inherited beliefs that shape attitudes at this important transition point, including the sense of loss and cessation of function as a woman which has been passed down through the generations – and which can unexpectedly strike at the heart of even the most ardent feminist, the dedicated career woman or the contented housewife. As well as having a conscious part of the mind, we all have a subconscious which holds on to old, often outdated, beliefs which we need to bring back into awareness, dust off and see how appropriate they are to our present life. These beliefs are usually very different to what we think we believe, and yet they may well be our strongest motivation and the source of our deepest fears. They are the basis for the conflicts and contradictions experienced during the menopause and may lie at the heart of some of the physical and emotional symptoms.

For many women, such as myself, these unsuspected beliefs remain hidden in the inaccessible parts of ourselves until they are triggered by the hormonal signals of the approaching menopause. This letter, from a contemporary who visited me during the writing of this book, shows just how potent these images can be:

> On the train journey back we got talking about the enduring myths around age and consequent self-imposed limitations. I recounted a short story by Alberto Moravia on this theme, which Sarah seemed to think you might find relevant to your menopause book.
>
> Very briefly, it tells of a man (a writer) married to a woman who is the joy and inspiration of his life, his dancing, graceful, beautiful muse. They share their house with the woman's elder sister who, by contrast, is taciturn, grim, and perennially dressed in black. On the woman's fortieth birthday the man buys his beloved wife a special gift, planning to give it to her at the celebratory dinner prepared for that night. But she arrives at the table garbed from head to toe in deepest black. With grief and despair, the man realizes that his precious darling is irretrievably lost to him. She believes forty marks the great divide, the shut-off point in her life as a woman. For her there is no alternative than to become a carbon copy of her dour sister.
>
> As I read this story many years ago, I'm pretty sure my telling of it is not completely exact. Unfortunately I don't remember its title, either, but if it does interest you, I'm sure you could easily find it in a collection of his stories.

I have not gone back to the original story, as it is the way the image stayed with her which I feel is relevant. Now that she has passed 'the great divide', somewhere in the depths of her subconscious mind, she is herself garbed in deepest black.

The changes connected with the menopause are not all negative. They include the possibility of fulfilling unused potential and thereby living a truly satisfying life, and the excitement of knowing ourselves as a person in our own right rather than as a mere appendage to our home, family or environment. Accessing a sense of purpose and creativity can empower regeneration and rebirth into new life for all women, but is particularly relevant during the rite of passage known as the menopause.

ABOUT THIS BOOK

This book offers practical ways of increasing well-being, including releasing from past patterns and alleviating physical symptoms. It looks at both 'conventional' and 'complementary' treatments for the symptoms of the menopause. It is not intending to 'sell' any one particular type of therapy, but rather to present information in a dispassionate way in order to allow the reader to make her own informed choice. It must be remembered that there is less hard scientific evidence in favour of the complementary therapies. This is only because they lack the backing of the powerful commercial vested interests which drive conventional research. On the other hand, some of the complementary therapies have been in use for hundreds and even thousands of years, and they are backed by generations of practical experience as to their efficacy and safety. It must also be borne in mind that this book, whilst giving some self-help measures, is offered as a guide only to these therapies and is not intended to replace the services of a physician or other qualified practitioner.

The book also explores the archetypal myths, seeking insights from the ancient wisdom sources, and celebrates the infinite possibilities open to 'women of a certain age'. It is especially appropriate for the pre-menopausal woman and those facing hysterectomy who wish to minimize physical discomfort and facilitate the rite of passage into the 'Wise Woman' phase of life, but post-menopausal women can derive equal benefit as it is never too late to become a truly Wise Woman. It will also be useful for health professionals who wish to understand the menopause more fully.

Designed as a workbook, the book encourages you to record, in the journal outlined in Chapter 3, your responses to various exercises which facilitate connection to, and expression of, your deepest feelings and beliefs. Not all the exercises will be relevant for you, although some may reveal unexpected reasons behind your symptoms or the crisis you may be experiencing in your life. You should work on the exercises that are appropriate. The important thing is that you should *do* the exercises that apply to you.

Merely thinking about them is not enough for a fundamental shift to take place. So please, do stop reading and take the time to work through each appropriate exercise as it arises, as it will lead you into the next stage of understanding and integrating your feelings. This will be a process that takes several months to complete. Allow yourself as much time as necessary before moving on to the next stage.

Almost inevitably, whilst you are exploring the depths of your emotions, you are going to go through a stage when you feel worse rather than better as things rise to the surface. Similarly, many alternative approaches to health provoke a physical 'healing crisis' (although I prefer the word 'challenge'), during which the body is throwing off its toxic load and consequently feels appalling. At such times you may well be tempted to give it all up, but do persevere as it will not last forever. If you can trust that this is a necessary stage your healing will be greatly enhanced. Your motto at this time should be, 'This too will pass'.

IS IT REALLY YOUR AGE?

Well, to a certain extent the answer has to be 'Yes', although that age can vary greatly and the same symptoms can affect women of pre-menopausal age who undergo a hysterectomy. *Menopause* literally means 'final cessation' and equates with the end of menstruation but the term is used to cover the time leading up to this event as well. At a certain stage in your life your body clock will gradually trigger certain hormonal changes which lead to cessation of ovulation and menstruation. Many of the physical and emotional symptoms of the menopause are caused by the fluctuating levels of hormones as the body tries to adapt to meet these changes. For women who take Hormone Replacement Therapy (HRT), the most usual symptom of the menopause, the cessation of bleeding, may be suspended indefinitely. There is no one 'right' time, nor would it appear that there is any such thing as a 'normal' menopause as individual experience varies widely.

Listen to your friends of similar age and note how many

times they use the phrase 'It's my age, you know' to excuse a wide variety of behaviour from forgetfulness to compulsive eating! Almost all menopausal women experience themselves as changing, becoming less able physically or mentally, and subject to certain irrational mood swings or outbursts of feeling from time to time.

There is some evidence that the degree of difficulty experienced with the menopause is culturally determined. In societies where the end of the menstruation signals new freedom, as in certain parts of India for instance, the menopause is a time of joy. On the other hand, American sociologist Pauline Burt carried out a study and found that middle-class Jewish mothers had the highest incidence of menopausal depression and it was suggested that this could be linked to the tendency to live life vicariously through their children. Conversely, in black communities where the grandmother lived with the family and cared for the children while the mother worked, there was very little incidence of menopausal depression.[5]

In the west, women have historically been taught to regard the menopause as an end so it is not surprising that it should produce some painful moments. The poet Keats, whilst not, I feel sure, writing specifically about the menopause, seems to sum up the pessimistic elements of change: regret, despair and loss:

> But were there ever any
>   Writh'd not at passing joy?
> To know the change and feel it,
> When there is none to heal it,
>   Nor numbed sense to steel it.

There is an optimistic face of change, however, one which is positive and constructive: forward-looking, anticipating unfoldment and expansion. If it can be viewed as one of the great rites of passage on a par with birth, death, puberty and marriage, then the menopause becomes a time of transition into a new phase of existence, a manifestation of the inherent feminine wisdom in every woman. It becomes a 'time of secret joy, spiritual growth, and super-exaltation' (Eliza Farnham).

SYMPTOMS

An incredibly diverse variety of symptoms has been reported in association with the menopause. These fall into two broad categories of 'physical' and 'emotional', although many are interlinked and some are mental; intermittent loss of memory, for instance, which provokes fears of premature senility. Whilst many of the symptoms are familiar to everyone, such as the ubiquitous and discomforting 'hot flush', many others, like back pain, are much more obscure and may well not be recognized as being symptomatic of the menopause unless a blood test is performed to check hormone levels. The full list has been included here not to frighten anyone, but rather because many women have found it reassuring to know that their experience is shared with others. Any unusual symptoms should, however, be checked by a physician.

It must be emphasized once again that not all women will experience symptoms, and only a very, very few will undergo the more debilitating and extreme effects. *The good news is that all symptoms are treatable* and need not make your life a physical and mental agony. And the even better news is that, once the menopause is over, women usually experience a new lease of life and much improved mental and physical energy levels.

Physical symptoms	**Emotional symptoms**
Hot flushes	Mood swings
Erratic periods	Depression
Flooding	Indecisiveness
Night sweats	Feelings of inadequacy
Aching bones, muscles or limbs	Extreme elation
Increased PMS	Anxiety
Tiredness/lethargy	Agitation
Headaches	Agoraphobia and other
Bloatedness	phobias
Insomnia	Tearfulness
Mastitis (tenderness of the breasts)	Changes in libido
Dizzy spells	Fearfulness
Vaginal dryness or discharge	Confusion
Weight gain	Vivid dreams
Back pain	Irritability

Physical symptoms
Hot or cold feet
Tingling or crawling of skin
Digestive problems
Flatulence
Gum disease and halitosis
Food allergies
Spots
Incontinence
Hair loss
Declining calcium levels
Decreasing or rising hormone
   levels
Palpitations
Cystitis
Prolapse
Osteoporosis
Arthritis
Cardiovascular changes
Vaginal infections, including
   thrush (candida)
Globus hystericus (a lump in the
   throat)

Emotional symptoms
Lack of energy
Irrational feelings
Loss of purpose
Being accident-prone

Mental symptoms
Loss of concentration
Loss of memory
Mental blanks
Occasional aphasia
   (inability to find the
   right word)
Confusion
Apprehension

THE CHANGE OR A LIFE CRISIS?

One of the difficulties in ascertaining how many of these symptoms, particularly the emotional ones, are directly linked to the menopause is that the forties and early fifties are often a period when there is a great deal of stress to cope with – a time of change when children or partners leave home, elderly parents may become a source of worry or even die, career decisions have to be taken, and partners too can be going through their own midlife crisis so that there is an overall lack of support available. Many 'new' women have been so busy building a career that they either haven't had time to have a family, or else have had to face considerable conflict and guilt over 'neglecting' their children (a particularly relevant issue in one-parent families where guilt is added to the stress of being the only decision-maker and source of discipline).

Others have come to childbearing relatively late,

suddenly realizing that 'time is slipping away, the biological clock is running out'. These women may well find that their daughters are entering puberty just as they enter the menopause (a situation which brings its own particularly poignant problems), or that they have to cope with the demands of very young children just at the time when their mental and physical energy seems to have reached an all-time low. In my counselling practice, I am consistently encountering women entering the forties who have found themselves face to face with an unexpected maternal urge. It is as though the body brings urgent pressure to bear, warning that it will soon be unable to fulfil its biological creative function. Other women have to confront the challenges and demands of their sexuality or life style. Each woman's experience is different, and yet there is a quintessential core which we share because we are Woman.

I asked a friend, who is now well into the Wise Woman phase of her life, to share her experience of the midlife years:

What a relief to be past the years of bodily change! But of course this is a misnomer, for the body changes, deteriorating with use as we go. In avoiding the word 'Menopause' – a vague time of life nevertheless easily identifiable – I have followed a pattern of thought established since childhood. It seemed to me, long ago, that easy excuses were given for different behaviour at several stages of life, adolescence, pre-menstrual and during pregnancy and after, to name but the most outstanding.

So I determined, as far as possible, to ignore the labels and get on with it, doffing my cap in passing recognition as I continued through life. I suppose the age of 47 saw 'The Change' ushered in unheralded, certainly unremarkable, but the major car accident in which I was the only injured victim, fortunately, left me glad that I was able to walk again, if painfully, after a year.

Remotivated, glad to be alive and mobile, I embarked on a three year course for teaching qualifications, in the middle of which my beloved mother was found to have cancer. She died a lingering death in the manner in which so many cancer victims have suffered.

Event piled upon event, but at last my husband and I settled down in the town we both liked, I with an attractive post at a good school. Two weeks later, after a road accident, my husband died. Life was changed again in a major way. The necessity of earning a living meant living and teaching at another school, bringing more pressures to cope with, in life's merry progress, for the next eight years.

Now, I haven't catalogued these events in a bid for sympathy. They are a fair summary of events that occur to most people at different times in their lives. But now, I wonder which comes first, the chicken or the egg?

There seems to be no doubt that life was meant to be a progression, often learning more thoroughly after suffering. This does not mean that prolonged suffering ennobles. Tragedies and difficulties in my life have meant that the more minor physical conditions were obscured, perhaps attributed to other physical causes such as concussion, or pelvic and bone injuries. What did happen was that my search for the deeper meaning of life and its purpose was intensified, continuing and satisfying in its contradiction of questioning, amazed awe at the magnitude of it all.

I've been fortunate. I can only hope that with the 'change of life' for each person, a profoundly deeper quality of life emerges.

So, the menopause may well get the blame when a life crisis is really at the root of the trouble. However, when viewed holistically, all stress or depression will affect your sense of well-being and, if you work through the relevant exercises in this book, you should be able to identify and change, or learn to accept, situations which are directly contributing to your present discomfort.

> Change is boundaries dissolved
> Space unlimited reaching stars
>
> Change is being lost in strange
> unrealness to end or begin
>
> Change is fear of things unknown
> approaching
>
> Change is water flowing under bridges
> a leaf carried by the flood to fortune
> or to oblivion
>
> Change is mourning for things ended
> regret for things undone now never to be known

Change is challenge to begin ever anew, a
letting go, renouncing, moving on

To find an unpredicted life now shaped.[6]

THE MEDICAL HISTORY OF THE MENOPAUSE[7]

Until the nineteenth century, menopause was not a medical
event. It was the province of herbalists and old wives and,
as such, treated as a natural part of life rather than a disease.
With the rise of a more monied, leisured class in the nineteenth century, women's health, or lack of it, began to be
taken over by the physicians and, ultimately, by the sur-
geons, virtually all of whom were, of course, male.

The Victorian gynaecologist Edward Tilt, writing in the
middle of the nineteenth century, saw the menopause as a
'gradual loss of feminine grace' leading to mental diseases,
morbid irrationality, minor forms of hysteria, melancholia,
an impulse towards drink and kleptomania and even
murder. The Change, in all its medical awe-fulness, had
arrived. Whilst Tilt advocated travelling and exercise as
beneficial, some of his treatment was almost as painful, and
toxic, as the symptoms he was trying to alleviate. He used
mineral water, sedatives, morphine, syrup of iron and potassium, bandaging of the limbs, and abdominal belts. But
his preferred method of treatment was bleeding. According
to Dr Tilt, menopausal disorders, and particularly the severe
headaches which often accompanied menopause, were due
to excessive blood stored in the head. So, Dr Tilt applied
leeches to the nape of the neck and behind the ears to
remove the noxious fluid.

By the 1890s, Dr Andrew Currier was still using leeches
but thought that bleeding was oldfashioned. He called Tilt
and his colleagues 'bleeders, pukers and purgers'. His preferred method of treatment was radical surgery: total
removal of the uterus and ovaries. If this did not remove
the symptoms, then the cause must be 'vicious habits, use
of alcohol, chloral, opium, etc.' or, even worse, 'excessive
sexual indulgence'. If all else failed, he blamed typhoid or
poverty. In Currier's view, early menopause was

socio-economic, the result of 'irregular and unwomanly occupations' such as being fishwives, metal workers, day labourers, cooks and laundresses. He described such women as 'pitiful spectacles of decrepit and wrinkled and worn out creatures at a period when the blush should still be on their cheeks', and, once again, advocated hysterectomy.

The notion of menopausal women as irrational and unstable really took off at the end of the century. Small wonder that in 1890 Alice James (sister of Henry and William), following a visit to the doctor for menopausal symptoms, commented: 'I suppose one has a greater sense of intellectual degradation after an interview with a doctor than from any other human experience'. A view that, unfortunately, many women could still empathize with today as the recently reported comment by an English (male) general practitioner shows: 'When they get to your age, women are supposed to rot'.[8]

The pioneer of psychoanalytic theory, Freud, saw the menopause as a time of potential crisis when previously undisturbed women could become quarrelsome and obstinate. And his follower Helene Deutsch developed the theory that menopause is the stage of life at which women's service to the species ends: menarche (the onset of menstruation) being the time when she becomes 'the servant of the species'. In other words, woman's usefulness is tied to her fertility and her life, such as it is, is over at menopause – a view which has been perpetuated for almost a century.

Surgery seems to have remained the preferred treatment for menopausal symptoms, certainly in America, until 1966 when oestrogen replacement therapy came in. However, it still remains the procedure of first resort for heavy bleeding.

Oestrogen was first isolated in 1923 by Allen and Doisey, who used the ovaries of sows. Following this, the most common source of oestrogen was the urine of pregnant mares. In 1966, oestrogen began to be used as a menopausal therapy. By the 1970s in the States, and the 1980s in Britain, hormone replacement therapy (HRT) was being hailed as the new 'cure-all': 'HRT keeps women out of the orthopaedic wards, the divorce courts and the mad house' (a consultant gynaecologist at a prestigious London hospital). In the foreword to *Forever Feminine* (an HRT manual) its author, Dr Wilson, was praised as 'a gallant knight come to rescue his fair lady not at the time of her bloom and flowering but in her despairing years'. However, as the authors of *The Curse* point out, 'in emphasizing a woman's breasts and her legs, rather than her intelligence and skills, the gallant knight reinforces the most destructive stereotypes in our sexist society.'

Unfortunately, much of the popular medical literature on HRT also emphasizes the aspect of avoiding the ageing process: *The Amarant Book of Hormone Replacement Therapy*[9] (from which the 'cure-all' quotation above was taken), for example, has a cover that proclaims 'HRT is the greatest treasure of a middle-aged woman's life. I've reached fifty but feel twenty . . .' The effect of such statements is to reinforce the middle-aged woman's tendency to hold back from becoming a mature, and inescapably older, woman. It is, in effect, saying: 'You only have a place in society if you retain the illusion of youth'. It contributes nothing to her inner development, and it leaves the control of her body firmly in the hands of the drug company and the prescribing physician, just as it has been in the hands of the gynaecological surgeon.

However, as many women have pointed out: 'Until women regain power over their bodies from the gynaecologists, they cannot own their power as a woman'. One way to regain this power over your own body is to make informed choices, based on objective information.

BIOLOGY IS NOT DESTINY[10]

For too long the function of a woman has been seen as an inferior role bounded by her fertility and capability as a mother. Even the feminist movement has, at times, seemed to subscribe to this view by apparently wanting to challenge and replace men rather than taking their natural place as a complement to them, with each bringing their own very special qualities and energies to the partnership.

For modern women to succeed past the menopause they have had to take on a masculine role in society. The former Prime Minister of England, Margaret Thatcher, is perhaps the ultimate example of this. Reputed to be on HRT (and thereby, metaphorically, still shedding her 'wise blood') the 'Iron Lady' has been a parody of both man- and woman-hood with her power dressing and openly flirtatious attitude to the, male, world leaders. She may well have been utilizing the post-menopausal rush of energy to give her her legendary stamina, but she did not integrate her femininity into her male role. Instead she was a mass of contradictions: dashing to be first on the scene at disasters to 'comfort' the victims, she nevertheless 'wholeheartedly' supported war. Gushing about the sanctity of the family, she did all in her power to destroy the supportive social and economic net-work that enabled that family to function. Nicknamed 'Thatcher the Milk Snatcher' in her first ministerial post, her political career was founded on being more heartless than any man.

Women who have reached the top in business, or the professions, have often found that they have had to be far more ruthless than their male colleagues, never for one moment showing any sign of feminine 'weakness' such as menstruation or sentiment. Most of them have had to bal-ance their needs as a woman against their need for 'success', and in almost every case have reached the top despite being female rather than because of it. The poet Rainer Maria Rilke saw this, from his 1934 viewpoint, as part of the transition into a new independent, separate and differen-tiated being: 'the feminine human'. He sees the intermediate stage as one in which 'the girl and the woman, in their new, their own unfolding, will but in passing be imitators of masculine ways and repeaters of masculine professions. After the uncertainty of such transitions it will become apparent that women were only going through the profusion and the vicissitude of those (often ridiculous) dis-guises in order to cleanse their most characteristic nature of the distorting influences of the other sex'.[11]

As Rilke suggests, women do have unique qualities to offer. The word 'blessing' comes from the Old English word *bloedsen* or 'bleeding' and indicates the intimate con-nection which has always existed between blood and religion. Blood was the link to the dark side of existence from which stemmed dreams and visions, and to the realm of magic and the numinous. Blood was often believed to be the vehicle for the spirit and woman's shedding of blood was inextricably linked to her mysterious capacity to create life. And, of course, it is the blood which carries the chemical messengers (including hormones) that regulate the biological functions of the body. In *The Great Cosmic Mother*, women are portrayed as the heart and core of ancient matriarchal society; menstruating and meditating together at the dark of the moon, intimately bonded by their shared blood rite, and thus ensuring the fertility and continuance of the sacred earth.

This situation was overthrown when the patriarchal religions moved in and menstrual taboos took over. At that time men, just as much as women, lost their participation in the mysteries and their connection with the earth. In ancient times, the horned god[12] was the consort of the goddess and male and female energies were united in the sacred marriage. The horned god was, voluntarily, given as an annual sacrifice for the good of the earth but he was replaced by a judgemental, vengeful, and presumably celibate, god who sacrificed his people. In this patriarchal society, the goddess and her consort were lost and women occupied an inferior role which was far from sacred, and their menstrual blood (that remnant of the goddess) became the subject for taboo. *Taboo* once meant 'set aside' (or holy) and therefore sacred; now it became synonymous with 'unclean' and therefore untouchable and inferior.

However, as the authors of *The Great Cosmic Mother* point out:

> It would seem that when there is no acknowledgement of women's bleeding, then there is instead a male acting-out of ritual and violent bloodshed in war. Warlike, aggressive male societies are in rivalry with women over which sex sheds the most sacred blood. War is men's response to women's ability to give birth and menstruate; all three are bloodshedding rituals. Women's blood rites give life, however, while men's bloody rituals give only death. To compensate for this, such authoritarian societies culturally repress and degrade women's blood functions, while elevating murderous war to a holy act. The women's menstrual 'mysteries of inspiration' become, in

war-god worshipping patriarchy, the 'mysteries of resisted knowledge' – repression, madness.[13]

Reading this on 15 January 1991, on the eve of what Saddam Hussein called 'the mother of all wars', had a profound effect on me. Saddam used many metaphors closely connected with the goddess (and, of course, Islam's emblem is the crescent moon, an age-old symbol of the goddess). He spoke of the 'ravens of savagery' (the Allied planes). In myth and fairy tale, the raven is the soul-bird who is a contact with the afterworld. This bird is intimately connected with death, resurrection and new life.

It had seemed to me for many years that mankind was hell-bent on destroying the planet and here was Saddam dealing out ecological disaster. I believed that only recognition of the Gaia 'earth-as-mother' concept could save humanity. Now, with the declaration of 'Holy War', in a battle fuelled by the 'masculine' attributes of greed and power, the sacrifice of human life became a blood rite and destruction was accelerating out of control. It became even more urgent that women, and in particular women who are retaining their 'wise blood' and therefore their creative, numinous power, should learn to recycle themselves from the scrap heap upon which they have been cast. 'It's in the blood' has a very particular and special meaning when it comes to feminine gnosis and it is possible to move back beyond the historical experience into a more primal knowing that honours and values the wisdom of the post-menopausal woman. A knowing that could, perhaps, save humanity from extinction:

> In woman is the form of all things,
> of all that lives and moves in the world.
> There is no jewel rarer than woman.
> There is not, nor has been, nor will be
> any destiny equal that of a woman.
>
> *Saktisangama Tantra*[14]

I. ✦ The Medical View

by Dr Robert Jacobs

Those 20% of women who suffer badly at menopause and perhaps some of the 60% who suffer mild symptoms are the women who present themselves at doctors' surgeries requesting help. Hence it is easy to see why the medical profession has adopted the attitude that menopause is a disease requiring treatment.[1]

Jane Lyttleton

In this chapter I intend to examine what western medical science has discovered about physiological and biochemical changes which take place in women's bodies at the time of the menopause. We will also look at the treatment options offered by contemporary western medicine for symptoms which can occur at the menopause, and certain medical conditions which can become more common following it.

In researching this book, I have been struck by the vast amount of scientific and medical information there is available on all matters concerning the menopause. There is even a monthly journal, *The Menopause Digest*, devoted entirely to abstracts of scientific papers on the menopause. When I mentioned this to an acquaintance of mine, she said: 'How come no one is telling women all this?' Indeed, this imbalance between the knowledge available to experts and the lack of readily accessible information for those who really need it, women, was what had surprised me. It is this imbalance which I hope to start redressing in this chapter.

While every effort has been made to ensure that the information presented here is correct at the time of writing, it must be borne in mind that information in this field is continually being updated as further research is carried out and new discoveries are made. Furthermore, there exist different schools of opinion on some medical aspects of the menopause, for instance the role of calcium supplements in preventing osteoporosis, and the length of time for which Hormone Replacement Therapy (HRT) should be given.

The term *menopause*, which is of Greek derivation, literally refers to the final menstrual period. Medically, the term *climacteric* is used to denote the complex of symptoms which can occur around the cessation of menstruation. In this chapter and the next I shall, for the sake of clarity, use the term *menopause* in its popular sense to mean the time surrounding the end of menstruation and the symptoms associated with it, rather than the more scientifically correct *climacteric*.

THE WESTERN MEDICAL VIEW

In western medicine, the principal event of the menopause is defined as 'primary ovarian failure'. This means that the female sex glands, the ovaries, cease functioning in that they no longer produce ova, or eggs, and no longer secrete sex hormones. The term 'primary ovarian failure' denotes that there is no cause for the ovaries to cease functioning other than the purely natural physiological changes due to ageing. It must also be remembered that in its medical and scientific use the word 'failure' is a neutral, descriptive term, referring to cessation of function, which carries with it none of the negative or judgemental connotations associated with the word 'failure' as used in everyday speech. In other words, the menopause is a natural physiological event and is not a disease. The term 'secondary ovarian failure' is reserved for cessation of ovarian function as a result of disease. We will not discuss this here as we are only concerned with the normal, natural, changes that occur at the time of the menopause.

The average age of women at menopause is fifty one. This figure has remained constant for as long as records have been kept. Of course, this is only an average figure and individual variations have always been noted. It has been speculated that the average age of the menopause may possibly be reduced in the near future as smoking is associated with an earlier onset of the menopause, and the habit of smoking is increasing among women at the present time, at least in western countries.

In the seventeenth century, only 28 per cent of women reached the menopause. Now, in the developed world, 95 per cent of women can expect to do so. This is due purely to increased life expectancy. A woman who is distressed by menopausal symptoms will probably not thank me, a man, for saying she does not know how lucky she is. Nevertheless, it is true that her great-grandmother would have had less chance of living long enough to experience the menopause.

Another interesting fact worth considering here is that the human female is the only mammal to experience a physical menopause. All other mammals are capable of reproduction up until the time of death. Thus the menopause, in common with writing, civilization and war, is one purely human aspect which separates us from the animals.

From the biological and evolutionary points of view, the reasons for this are clear. Human infants need an extended period of nurturing and education before they are mature enough to fend for themselves. So if women were able to reproduce up until the time of death, there would be a large number of helpless orphans still requiring eighteen years of nurturing, who would have to be cared for by other members of the community. This problem does not occur in the animal kingdom where, for instance, young horses can run almost as soon as they are born.

The fact that humans alone experience a menopause also implies that, from a biological and evolutionary point of view, *human females of post-reproductive age are necessary for the functioning of human societies.* So, women who are themselves beyond the age of childbearing have accumulated wisdom and skills which they can pass on to younger women and to society in general. The biological fact that, alone of all mammals, a woman can have twenty or thirty useful years, or one-third of her life, after ceasing to reproduce would seem to give the lie to Helene Deutsch's view, quoted earlier, that women are useful to society only when they can reproduce. On the contrary, nature has seen fit to ensure that women do survive beyond their reproductive years in a useful capacity.

PHYSIOLOGICAL CHANGES

Before menopause, the ovaries, or sex glands, produce female sex hormones or oestrogens. At the time of the menopause, there is a reduction in the level of circulating oestrogens. This lowering in the level of oestrogens causes the pituitary gland, situated at the base of the brain, to secrete increased quantities of hormones known as gonadotrophins. In the pre-menopause woman, gonadotrophins have the effect of causing the ovaries to produce oestrogen. After the menopause, the level of gonadotrophins rises in what can be seen as a vain physiological attempt to keep the ovaries functioning. Measurement of gonadotrophin levels provides the only sure-fire medical test to determine whether the menopause has definitely occurred. If the ratio of FSH to LH (Follicle Stimulating Hormone to Luteinizing Hormone – two types of gonadotrophin) is greater than three, then ovarian function has ceased and the woman can definitely be said to be post-menopausal.

The main type of oestrogen present prior to the menopause is known as oestradiol. The main sex hormone present post-menopause is oestrone. This is due to the fact that the adrenal glands, as well as the ovaries, produce sex hormones and they carry on doing so after the menopause. The adrenal glands produce a hormone (with the lovely name of dehydroepiandrosterone) which is converted to oestrone in the body's fat stores. This probably explains the fact that plump women tend to have fewer menopausal symptoms than thin ones. This is the only known medical advantage to being overweight!

The reduction in oestrogen levels can lead to a number of different symptoms being experienced at the time of the menopause. Different women vary in the severity and amount of symptoms they experience. The following are some of the medically recognized symptoms or physiological changes that can be experienced at or around the menopause:

Hot flushes	Insomnia	Osteoporosis
Sweats	Apprehension	Cardiovascular
Dizziness	Headaches	changes

Globus hystericus (a lump in the throat)	Anxiety	Urge incontinence
Formication (crawling sensation in the skin)	Libido changes	Arthropathies (painful joints)
	Loss of concentration	Skin atrophy
	Depression	

Of the above list of symptoms, only the hot flushes (or hot flash as it is called in the USA) is a uniquely menopausal symptom. All the other symptoms can occur also in situations unrelated to the menopause.

There is some evidence of cultural variation of menopausal symptoms, although one recent study showed that women living in rural Africa had very similar symptoms to women living in developed countries. This suggests that menopausal symptoms have a physiological and not a purely cultural basis.

The commonest symptoms are hot flushes and sweating. These are experienced by 75 per cent of women. At one time it was assumed that hot flushes were a purely subjective or psychological phenomenon. This, however, has been demonstrated to be untrue. Measurements have been made of physiological changes which occur in the bodies of women during hot flushes. These show an increase in finger temperature due to expansion of blood vessels in the skin and an increase in heart rate. This shows that the hot flush is a genuine physical event and not a psychological one.

The mean duration of a hot flush is three minutes, although they can last for anything between 0.5 and sixty minutes. The weekly number experienced can vary from one to a hundred. No trigger factors have been medically recognized as setting off hot flushes. Following a hot flush, sweating often occurs and this may be followed by evaporation and a feeling of chills.

The exact cause of hot flushes is not known, although it would seem to relate to declining levels of oestrogen in the blood. Hot flushes occur more commonly where the menopause has been induced surgically by removal of the ovaries as a result of disease. This suggests that the rate of fall of the level of oestrogen is important in determining whether hot flushes occur or not. Hot flushes are more likely to be experienced when there is a sudden drop in oestrogen levels than when there is a gradual reduction over a period of time.

Palpitations and dizziness are fairly common symptoms, occurring in more than half of menopausal women. Formication, which refers to a sensation similar to that of insects crawling over the skin (from the Latin *formica* – an ant) is a reasonably common but unexplained symptom which occurs in approximately a third of menopausal women. Indigestion can occur fairly commonly at the time of the menopause. Globus hystericus, or the sensation of a lump in the throat, is a rare menopausal symptom. It is presumed to be psychological in origin and occurs more commonly in situations other than the menopause. It is, however, easily dealt with by means of a homoeopathic remedy (see Chapter 3).

ANXIETY AND DEPRESSION

Anxiety and depression may complicate the menopause. Statistically speaking, there is an increase in psychological problems in pre-menopausal women aged between forty five and forty nine, compared with younger women. This statistical increase continues for one year after the menopause and then the incidence of psychiatric problems drops sharply to less than it is in younger women. This is good news for all women currently struggling with menopausal difficulties. It is important to realize that a period of tranquillity lies ahead and that symptoms do get better.

The reason for the increased incidence of anxiety and depression is not clear. It may be a part of the menopause or it may be secondary to it. It may have social causes. Our society does not particularly value women of post-menopausal years and they have no clearly defined role, and a woman may fear the perceived loss of social status. At the same time, a woman's children are likely to be growing up and leaving home, leaving her feeling less valued. There may be conflict with adolescent children, or a woman's husband may be undergoing his own midlife crisis.

Western medicine recognizes two kinds of depression which may occur at the menopause. The first is known as Reactive Depression; this usually accompanies a situation of stress within the family. Disturbances of appetite and sleep are uncommon in this sort of depression. The sufferer feels better for happy events and removal of the stressful situation. Typically symptoms are better after waking in the morning and get worse as the day goes on. Psychotherapy and counselling may help this type of depression.

The second type of menopausal depression is called Endogenous Depression. This would appear to have more of a biochemical basis. The sufferer typically feels worse in the mornings and make awake early. Happy events do not cheer up the sufferer. This type of depression is most likely to respond to antidepressant drugs, of which a large number of extremely effective ones are now available.

Anyone suffering from menopausal depression should bear in mind that, as stated earlier, once the menopause is over the chance of experiencing depression becomes much less than it is for younger women.

Vaginal dryness and atrophy may occur due to the reduced levels of oestrogen. The trigone of the bladder (that part of the urinary bladder which is most sensitive, and where the greater part of the nerve endings are situated) may also be affected and this can lead to urge incontinence. This is a sudden desire to pass urine which may then leak out. Both of these distressing symptoms may respond to HRT, which is discussed later in the chapter.

It is always important to bear in mind that, although the symptoms occurring at the time of the menopause may be unpleasant, none of them has any significant mortality associated with it. In other words, none of them has ever proved fatal and all are treatable.

PSYCHOSEXUAL PROBLEMS

Psychosexual problems may occur during the menopause. While vaginal dryness is well known, it does not seem to be the principal cause of problems and, in any case, may be easily treated.

Loss of libido can occur and would seem to be caused, at least in part, by psychological and social factors. A recent study of menopausal women suffering from loss of libido found that such women were more likely to be married and their husbands more likely to suffer from erectile impotence. Many of the women, when questioned, stated that although they thought an active sex life was important for their husband, they thought it less important for them, as they themselves were not particularly interested. Many of the women questioned felt guilty about the loss of libido and still had intercourse for their husband's sake. This in turn may have added to their guilt and resentment and have helped to compound their loss of libido.

It was found that women who experienced loss of libido were more likely to suffer from anorgasmia (apparent lack of ability to have an orgasm) than women who did not. Of course, anorgasmia is not confined solely to menopausal women.

It has also been observed that dryness of the vagina is unrelated to loss of libido, suggesting that loss of libido is not related to oestrogen deficiency. This fits in with the observation that loss of libido responds less well to HRT than do some of the other menopausal symptoms, although in a percentage of cases it may respond.

All this would suggest that the more one has developed a satisfying and fulfilling sex life prior to the menopause, the more likely one is to enjoy a satisfying sex life after it. It would also suggest that psychosexual counselling may be appropriate for loss of libido at the menopause, as at least part of the cause may be psychological.

Loss of libido in menopausal women has been found to respond, in a certain percentage of cases, to the administration of androgens (or male sex hormones, a certain amount of which are present in all women, just as all men possess a certain amount of oestrogens, or female sex hormones). This, and other therapeutic options, will be looked at in more detail later in the chapter.

POST-MENOPAUSAL CONDITIONS AND PREVENTIVE MEASURES

So far we have looked at the changes which can occur around the time of the menopause. Now I wish to consider those changes which can affect women who have already gone through the menopause. Compared to pre-menopausal women, women who are post-menopausal are at an increased risk of both heart disease and osteoporosis ('thinning of the bones'). It is important to look at these in some detail as many practical steps can be taken to reduce the risk of these conditions. The chances of both conditions occurring are also reduced by HRT. A regular programme of exercise has also been shown to reduce significantly the occurrence of both. Other life style changes also have an appreciable effect on the incidence of these conditions.

HEART DISEASE

Prior to the menopause, women are far less likely to suffer from heart disease than are men. After the menopause, the incidence among women rises so that it equals that among men of the same age. This is reflected in the fact that post-menopausal women have higher levels of cholesterol and low-density lipoproteins (those blood fats associated with coronary artery disease) than do pre-menopausal women, and this leads to the higher incidence of coronary artery disease.

The exact mechanism of this is unclear but it would seem probable that oestrogens have a protective effect against heart disease by helping to maintain low levels of cholesterol and blood fats. Indeed, prior to the menopause, oestrogens are manufactured by the body from cholesterol, and so the cessation of their manufacture at the menopause probably leads to an excess of unused cholesterol.

It has been shown that HRT apparently reduces the incidence of heart disease in post-menopausal women. It has also been shown that exercise has a beneficial effect on preventing heart disease in women after the menopause. The exercise needs to be aerobic; that is, it needs to be done continuously at a sustained elevated heart rate, so it has to be reasonably brisk. In order to reduce the risk of heart disease, without incurring the risk of significant injury, women need to exercise for thirty minutes at a time, three times a week.

Other steps that can be taken to reduce the risk of heart disease include stopping smoking, maintaining normal body weight and eating a diet high in natural fibre and low in animal fats. The consumption of fish oils and olive oil has also been shown to have a beneficial effect on the incidence of heart disease.

OSTEOPOROSIS

Osteoporosis, or 'thinning of the bones', is the most significant consequence of the ovaries ceasing to function.

Osteoporosis is a condition where the bone is normally mineralized, but the overall volume of bone tissue per volume of bone is reduced. In other words, the bones do become 'thin' rather than just having a reduced amount of calcium. The consequences are pathological fractures (fractures occurring spontaneously or from a trivial injury), principally of the hip, spine and wrist. This is a serious cause of injury in elderly women.

The increased incidence of osteoporosis after the menopause is thought to be due to declining levels of oestrogen. Chemical receptors for oestrogens have been demonstrated in bone. An increase in the activity of osteoclasts (cells which break down bone) has also been shown after the menopause. The osteoclasts are stimulated by a chemical whose action, before the menopause, is normally blocked by oestrogen.

However, it is important to bear in mind that *not all women get osteoporosis after the menopause.* In fact, there are a number of well-recognized risk factors associated with an increased incidence of osteoporosis:

Risk factors for osteoporosis

Reduced height for weight ratio
Family history of osteoporosis
Early menopause
Low calcium intake
Being of Caucasian descent
Nulliparity (having had no children)
High alcohol intake

High caffeine intake
Heavy smoking
Lack of physical activity

The reduced height for weight ratio reflects the fact that one of the earliest signs of osteoporosis may be a reduction in height due to compression of the vertebrae or bones of the spine.

The standard American textbook on gynaecology, and one of the best in the world, *Novak's Textbook of Gynecology*,[2] gives an interesting picture of women who are at risk of suffering from osteoporosis. It describes the population at risk as 'women who have always been thin with little subcutaneous fat, who are heavy smokers and who eat a high protein diet, or a junk-food diet with soft drinks and a low consumption of dairy products. They are sedentary and have little exposure to sun.'

So we can see that there are a number of steps one can take to reduce one's risk of osteoporosis. These include cutting out smoking and not drinking too much tea or coffee, and a diet containing adequate amounts of calcium but not too much red meat, as the excessive consumption of red meat can interfere with the absorption of calcium from the gut. On these steps to prevent osteoporosis the thinking of 'conventional' medicine would seem to be very much in tune with that of the 'natural' health movement.

The role of calcium supplements in preventing osteoporosis is unclear. Different scientific studies have come up with different results. A recent study showed that, where the dietary intake of calcium is above 500 mg per day, calcium supplements make no difference to bone mass. This means that it is of no value except in areas such as China where the average calcium intake is low. Some studies have shown that in post-menopausal women, supplementation of between 1500 mg and 2000 mg per day reduces bone loss, while other studies have not confirmed this. So, while even the experts differ about the usefulness of calcium supplements, it would be sensible to ensure that one's diet contains adequate amounts of calcium.

In the west, the single greatest source of calcium in the diet is dairy products, and the second is fish such as sardines eaten with their bones. Cultures which do not consume a lot of dairy products often have an alternative source of calcium. For instance, tahini (ground sesame seeds) is an extremely calcium-rich (and delicious) food which is used in the Middle East.

The following are some of the foods which contain calcium:

Parmesan cheese	Sesame seeds	Cheddar cheese	Carob powder
Tuna	Sardines	Salmon	Parsley
Spinach	Broccoli	Haricot and	Tofu
Figs	Brazil nuts	lima beans	Milk
Egg yolks	Rhubarb	Yoghurt	

Of this list, Parmesan cheese, sesame seeds and Cheddar cheese contain by far the greatest amount of calcium per weight of food.

Perhaps the single most effective thing a woman can undertake herself to reduce her risk of osteoporosis is a programme of regular exercise. It has been shown that regular exercise can prevent bone loss in post-menopausal women. We saw earlier that the type of exercise needed to prevent heart disease was aerobic, which accelerates the heart rate. By contrast, the best sort of exercise to prevent osteoporosis is isometric exercise, in which tension is increased in groups of muscles. So jogging would be an example of aerobic exercise and weight-lifting would be an example of isometric exercise.

Obviously the ideal exercise for the post-menopausal woman would be one that is both aerobic and isometric.[3] The best example of such an exercise is swimming. This has the dual effect of raising heart rate and working on all the muscle groups. The importance of exercising different muscle groups is that they pull on the bones and so help strengthen them. However, in order to reduce the risk of fractures of the hip, the most potentially serious consequence of osteoporosis, exercise needs to be weightbearing, such as dancing, skipping or walking, so such activities should be included in a programme of regular exercise.

Yoga is a good example of an isometric exercise. If done vigorously, it can also be aerobic. The Chinese 'soft' martial art T'ai Chi Ch'uan is an exercise which activates all of the body's muscle groups and also significantly accelerates heart rate. Besides which, it also confers self-defence skills, useful for a woman to have whatever her age. The oriental forms of exercise can also give a feeling of mental well-being that not all western forms of exercise provide.

Perhaps the most important thing about a programme of exercise is that it should be something you enjoy doing so that it does not become a chore. If you already have a sport which you enjoy, by all means continue with it. It is a good thing to cultivate a more generally energetic life style. Try walking or cycling to the shops, leaving the car in the garage, so at the same time benefiting yourself and making less of a contribution to the 'greenhouse effect'.

It is probably not a good idea for someone in middle age who is unused to exercise suddenly to take up a very vigorous exercise like jogging: a brisk daily walk would be a good introduction or even a substitute.

There is evidence that the greater one's peak bone mass (which depends to some extent on exercise and calcium intake *before* the menopause), the lower one's chances of getting osteoporosis. This means that it is never too soon to start exercising and ensuring an adequate calcium intake, no matter how young one is. As fracture of the hip and its complications secondary to osteoporosis is the twelfth commonest cause of death in the USA, it is worth even adolescent girls being aware of preventive steps against osteoporosis. As one Australian researcher recently put it, 'A daily glass of milk and a walk would save $100,000 a year'.[4]

It is known that bone loss commences as soon as the ovaries stop functioning, so don't delay, start exercising!

It is also clear that HRT prevents bone loss, although this recommences as soon as the treatment is stopped.

HORMONE REPLACEMENT THERAPY (HRT)

As previously mentioned, HRT as a treatment for symptoms of the menopause was first used in 1966 in the USA. Initially, oestrogen replacement was given on its own but, by 1975, it had become apparent that there was a link between oestrogen replacement therapy and endo-metrial carcinoma (cancer of the lining of the womb). It was established, however, that if progestogens (another type of hormone present in the pre-menopausal female) were added as well, there was then no increased risk of cancer of the womb. Indeed, a recent study showed that if progestogen is given the risk of endometrial cancer is less than if no HRT is given at all, although, in any case, its incidence is rare. So today oestrogen is given cycli-cally, with progestogen being added for at least ten days of the cycle. A break in treatment of one week is left between cycles, during which 'withdrawal' bleeding occurs. This is the form administered in the UK at the present time.

Some menopausal symptoms respond better to HRT than others. Symptoms like hot flushes and night sweats show the greatest improvement, but many others also respond. Among the symptoms which may improve are impairment of memory, depression, irritability, anxiety, vaginal dryness, urinary frequency and urge incontinence. Of women with hot flushes, some 77 per cent respond to HRT although this figure includes a placebo effect – just talking about one's problem can be beneficial – which may account for as much as 30 per cent of the improvement.

HRT does not appear to be particularly beneficial for loss of libido. One study showed only a 2 per cent improvement in patients with loss of libido, while another study showed a 12 per cent improvement.

Some 34 per cent of cases of anxiety and depression have been shown to respond to HRT, although depression on its own is not considered an indication for HRT.

This all suggests that if your main complaints at the menopause are hot flushes and a dry vagina, you are more likely to be helped by HRT than if your main complaints are lethargy and loss of libido.

There are, however, a number of well-recognized contra-indications to HRT. These fall into two categories: absolute contra-indications and relative contra-indications:

Contra-indications to HRT

Absolute	*Relative*
Breast carcinoma	Previous heart attack
Endometrial carcinoma	Previous stroke
Endometrial hyperplasia	Abnormal blood lipids (fats)
	Thrombo-embolic disease (e.g. deep vein thrombosis or pulmonary embolism)
	Breast dysplasia
	Acute liver disease
	Obesity
	Heavy smoking
	Oestrogen-dependent pelvic disease (fibroids, endometriosis)
	Strong family history of breast cancer

Most authorities agree that HRT should not be given at all to patients with a history of conditions which appear in the list of absolute contra-indications. These are carcinoma of the breast, carcinoma of the endometrium (or lining of the womb), and endometrial hyperplasia which is a benign enlargement of the lining of the womb, but which risks turning malignant if HRT is given. One leading British authority, however, has recently argued that even women with a history of these conditions should be allowed to make an informed choice as to whether to have HRT or not.

As far as the conditions which are listed as relative contra-indications are concerned, no definite hazard with HRT has been proved but there is sufficient circumstantial evidence to warrant a specialist's opinion in these cases as to whether it is advisable to give HRT or not.

It is considered that HRT is best avoided in those with a history of heart attacks, strokes or pulmonary embolism (a blood clot in the blood vessels of the lung). However, if menopausal symptoms are very severe it may be prescribed under close medical supervision.

Regarding abnormal levels of blood fats (or lipids), if there is a family history of abnormal blood fats (congenital hyperlipidaemia), then HRT should *not* be given. However, this is a very rare condition. If there is a raised cholesterol level but no family history, then the position is unclear, but it is likely that there is no risk in taking HRT.

In the case of breast dysplasia (benign nodular lumps in the breast) then mammography is indicated before starting HRT.

Acute liver disease is a contra-indication. No HRT should be given for a year after an attack of hepatitis.

In the case of high blood pressure this should be reduced to normal before starting HRT. Then there is no risk.

Where high blood pressure, obesity and smoking co-exist, there is a risk in using HRT. The lowest possible dose should be used and the patient should stop smoking and lose weight.

Diabetes is not a contra-indication to HRT providing that it is well controlled.

Regarding oestrogen-dependent pelvic disease (fibroids and endometriosis), HRT may make fibroids bigger and increased withdrawal bleeding is a problem. HRT can exaggerate the symptoms of endometriosis (an abnormal but benign proliferation of the lining of the womb into sites where it does not normally occur) but these get better once treatment is stopped.

Some authorities believe that HRT should not be given if there is a strong family history of breast cancer, though there is not complete agreement on this.

SIDE EFFECTS OF HRT

Besides the clearly defined contra-indications to HRT, there are also a number of side effects associated with it. As HRT has to be given cyclically, withdrawal bleeding occurs between cycles. The bleeding is less than a normal period but some women find it unacceptable, especially if they have been without periods for a while. However, a combined HRT pill has recently been developed which does not cause withdrawal bleeding. As this drug is very new, it is still being closely monitored for adverse side effects.

Some women fear that, if they are still bleeding, they may get pregnant and need to be reassured that this is not the case. Pregnancy cannot occur once normal periods have stopped but contraception is usually advised for at least a year after the last period. On the other hand, *HRT is not a contraceptive* (the doses of hormones are less than in 'the pill') so if a woman is still having periods, barrier methods of contraception should be used.

Like 'the pill', HRT carries with it certain 'nuisance effects'. These can include tenderness of the breasts, and if a woman has previously suffered from Pre-Menstrual Syndrome (PMS), it may return. Some women complain that they just do not feel 'normal' on HRT and are unable to tolerate it on account of such non-specific side effects. (My co-author had this problem with HRT which indirectly led to this book being written!)

Some women fear weight gain with HRT. In fact, the average weight gain on starting HRT is only 0.5 kg and weight tends to increase around the menopause anyway.

Transient nausea is sometimes experienced on commencing HRT but this usually wears off in a short time.

Besides being effective against menopausal symptoms, HRT also has a protective effect against heart disease and strokes, as mentioned earlier. This is especially the case if 'natural' rather than synthetic oestrogens are used. ('Natural' oestrogens are derived from horses rather than being made in the laboratory.)

HRT also protects against the development of osteoporosis as discussed earlier. HRT has been found to reduce the incidence of pathological fractures by 60 per cent and this alone is a big argument in its favour. We have seen, however, that other factors besides HRT have a benign influence on the risk of osteoporosis.

OTHER THERAPIES FOR MENOPAUSAL CONDITIONS

Certain studies have shown that the administration of androgens (male sex hormones such as testosterone) can have a beneficial effect on loss of libido. One study showed that giving a mixture of androgens and oestrogens had a more significant effect on libido than giving oestrogen alone. As mentioned earlier, male sex hormones are a normal part of a woman's physiology. Testosterone has to be given by implantation under the skin as it is not absorbed by mouth. This therapy has, however, been known to give rise to unwanted side-effects of masculinization. For instance, an increased growth of facial hair and a permanent deepening of the voice have been known to occur. Other approaches to this problem are discussed later in the book.

Hot flushes have also been shown to respond to administration of the hormone Norethisterone which is not an oestrogen but a progestogen.

The drug Etidronate Disodium, which is a Biphosphonate compound, appears to have a beneficial effect on the development of osteoporosis. Recent studies have shown that post-menopausal osteoporosis can even be reversed using subcutaneous implants of oestradiol which produce high oestrogen levels.

Topical application of oestrogen-containing creams may help vaginal dryness, especially the atrophic vaginitis which can occur in elderly women and which may be distressing, but some absorption of oestrogen into the bloodstream can occur. Non-medicated lubricants may also be useful in vaginal dryness.

PROGNOSIS

If left untreated, symptoms such as hot flushes generally last from one to five years. Up to now it has been usual to continue HRT for about eighteen months, and longer if symptoms recur after that time. There is a growing school of opinion in favour of continuing HRT for a much longer period, especially in view of the beneficial effects in preventing heart disease and osteoporosis.

However, there is at present an on-going debate over how long HRT should be continued. Two leading British authorities recently advocated continuing HRT for ten years.[5] They argue that ten years' therapy would delay the onset of osteoporosis sufficiently to prevent it being a problem in later life; it would also protect the cardiovascular system from heart attacks or strokes. They also say that they see no reason for a woman not to continue HRT indefinitely if she wishes to do so. They do, however, point out that not all women are prepared to put up with monthly bleeding or the side effects mentioned earlier, and admit that many women will decide for themselves when to stop having HRT. Other authorities, however, adopt a more cautious attitude towards long-term HRT, arguing that at present too little is known about the effects of its long-term administration.

This chapter represents a summary of the present state of knowledge of the menopause and HRT. It is important to remember that this is being updated all the time, and what is considered correct practice now may not be so in five years' time. On the negative side, this means that treatments which appear perfectly safe when first introduced may turn out to have certain drawbacks which only become apparent after some time. On the positive side, it means that treatments are likely to become refined and updated as more research is done.

SUMMARY

1.   The menopause is defined in western medicine as primary ovarian failure. This means that the ovaries cease producing oestrogen.
2.   There are a number of symptoms associated with the menopause, the majority of which can respond to HRT.
3.   The two main health problems associated with the post-menopausal state are heart disease and osteoporosis.
4.   HRT can help to prevent both these conditions, as does a regular regime of exercise.

2. 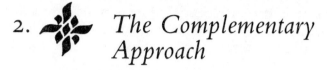 The Complementary Approach

by Dr Robert Jacobs

Menopause is a naturally occurring transition. As a physiological event it is not a disease and it need not be accompanied by any discomfort.[1]

Honora Lee Wolfe

In this chapter we will look at the treatment of the symptoms associated with the menopause from the point of view of so-called 'complementary' or 'alternative' therapies. What these therapies have in common is that they all make use of naturally occurring, rather than synthetic substances, and that they all utilize the human organism's own capacity to heal itself. I use the term 'organism' to mean not just the physical body but also the subtle bio-energetic regulatory mechanisms associated with it, and the far subtler energies of mind and spirit.

One other property these therapies have in common is age. Homoeopathy, for instance, is some hundreds of years old, while herbalism and Chinese medicine have a history going back thousands of years. These therapies also treat the human organism as one whole, as opposed to modern western medicine which concentrates on treating the specific effects of disease.

As stated in the Introduction, it must be remembered that there is less available hard scientific evidence in favour of these therapies. This is only because the complementary therapies lack the backing of the powerful commercial vested interests, in the form of pharmaceutical companies and the chemical industry, which provide the funds to pay for conventional research. There is no incentive for them to research or promote the therapeutic properties of a naturally occurring herb, as a herb cannot be patented. A chemical substance, on the other hand, can be patented. Therefore, conventional research, driven by the profit motive, is led mainly to research the therapeutic properties of synthetic chemicals. When it does investigate natural substances, it is in order to synthesize them: that is, to manufacture them artificially.

By the same token, powerful voices within the medical profession and the pharmaceutical industry decry the 'complementary' therapies as hopelessly lacking in scientific basis, conveniently ignoring what scientific work has been done, largely by interested individuals, and the fact that generations of experience attest to their efficacy and safety. This in turn leads to a backlash by the supporters of 'natural' medicine, many of whom regard all conventional therapies as over-invasive or too dangerously toxic to use at all. This attitude also ignores the genuine advances made by conventional medicine and its great usefulness in many conditions, especially in acute life-threatening ones.

I regard this polarization of attitudes as particularly unfortunate as it divides those working in the therapeutic field into two opposing groups who generally do not communicate, but who would have a lot to learn from each other if they did. I am reminded of the words spoken at a seminar I attended on Tibetan medicine led by Dr Wangyal, a renowned doctor of traditional Tibetan medicine and former personal physician to His Holiness the Dalai Lama. He said: 'There should be no conflict between Eastern medicine and Western medicine, nor between "conventional" medicine and "alternative" medicine, as all systems of medicine have their own advantages and their own limitations.'

This typically broadminded Tibetan view (it is worth noting that, in the Tibetan medicinal system, closed-mindedness is regarded as one of the causes of disease) shows a very enlightened attitude that can pave the way for a truly holistic form of medicine combining the best features of many different systems. Thus the therapies mentioned below can be used alongside conventional treatment if necessary, as well as in combination with each other.

Again, I must state that the information presented here is only a guide to what is available and is not intended to replace the services of a physician or other qualified practitioner. You are strongly advised to seek the services of an experienced and qualified practitioner for any complementary therapy. The addresses of practitioners in your area can be obtained from the registers of the governing bodies listed under each therapy in 'Useful Addresses' in the back of this book. I should also perhaps mention that I have selected only a small number of the complementary therapies that are available. These are the ones which I and my co-author can recommend from personal experience. However, other approaches, such as aromatherapy and reflexology, may also prove beneficial in relieving symptoms.

WESTERN HERBAL MEDICINE

In the last chapter we looked at modern western medicine, so it is appropriate to start here by looking at the system of complementary medicine most similar to modern western medicine, and which may be regarded as its ancestor. This is Western Herbalism.

For thousands of years our ancestors made use of the natural healing properties of plants. The therapeutic methods of ancient Greece, Rome, and medieval Europe would have consisted almost entirely of herbal medicine. Contemporary western herbal medicine derives from these sources and from European folk medicine, together with some input from other herbal traditions, such as that of the North American Indian. It is worth noting that the only medical book taken by the Pilgrim Fathers on their voyage to the New World was Culpeper's *Herbal* and that for the first 200 years of its existence, the principal form of medicine practised in what was to become the USA was herbalism.

A large proportion of the drugs used in conventional western medicine ultimately have plant origins. Examples include the opiate group of painkillers (Morphine, Codeine) and the digitalis group of heart drugs and some anti-asthma drugs (Theophylline, Ephedrine). Even the antibiotics are ultimately of plant, albeit fungal, origin. Pharmaceutical research tends to isolate one particular active chemical from a herb that may contain several. For instance, the anti-asthma drug Ephedrine is isolated from the Chinese herb Ma Huang (*Ephedra sinica*). Although effective against asthma, Ephedrine has side effects of increasing heart rate and raising blood pressure. The whole herb, however, also contains the alkaloid pseudo-ephedrine which lowers blood pressure as well as relieving asthma. This means that, when given therapeutically, the entire herb has little or no effect on blood pressure. In fact, Ma Huang contains twenty five alkaloids as active ingredients, but conventional medicine makes use of only one of them. Thus, many herbs may be safer to use and have fewer side effects than chemicals derived from the same herbs. This is just one of the advantages of using herbal medicine.

Some herbs can be obtained already made up into pill form, but the commonest way of taking herbs is as a decoction, an infusion or a tincture. A decoction, is prepared by boiling the herb with water, an infusion is prepared by adding boiling water to it, in order to make a tea or liquid extract. A tincture is prepared by soaking the herbs in alcohol, or a mixture of alcohol and water, so that an alcoholic extract is obtained. Suppliers of tinctures and raw herbs are listed at the back of this book, although once again I should state that a qualified practitioner should be consulted.

We shall now examine some of the herbs commonly used in the West which may be of value in the menopause.

AGNUS CASTUS

Possibly the most useful of all herbs for dealing with the menopause, Agnus castus has a long history. It was used by Athenian matrons in classical times to strew in their beds. It was also used in the rites of Ceres, or Demeter, the goddess of the harvest, which were celebrated at Eleusis.[2] It was eaten by monks in the Middle Ages as a condiment, the seeds being ground up and sprinkled on their food. The purpose of this was to help them to observe their vows of chastity, hence its alternative names of Chaste Tree and Monks Pepper.[3]

Pharmacologically, Agnus castus contains oestrogen-like

substances and also has a normalizing effect on hormone production, especially that of progesterone. It is sometimes said to have an amphoteric effect. This means that it appears to have two different and opposing actions, so it has a reputation as both an aphrodisiac and an anaphrodisiac. This is simply explained by its ability to normalize hormone levels. Its anaphrodisiac effects occur in males and are explained by its oestrogenic properties. The same properties make it a very useful herb for the menopause as it functions rather like an 'organic' hormone replacement therapy.

The active parts of the plant are the berries which are used in a dosage of 3–6 g (or 1–2 ml of the tincture) three times a day. It is also readily available in a number of proprietary herbal preparations intended for use during the menopause, which are obtainable from health food shops without the need for a prescription.

Women who do not wish to have conventional HRT, or are unable to tolerate it, may well find that Agnus castus provides an excellent substitute. (It is highly recommended by my co-author Judy Hall.)

RED SAGE
Salvia officinalis

Like Agnus castus, Salvia also has a history going back to ancient times. There is a Latin proverb, *Cur moriatur homo cui Salvia crescit in horto* ('Why should a man die while sage grows in his garden?'). This is reflected in the medieval English proverb: 'He that would live for aye must eat Sage in May'. Buckinghamshire folklore records that the wife rules the household when Sage grows vigorously in the garden. Perhaps this reflects Sage's affinity with the female sex and their problems, a property reflected also in the medieval astrologers' assigning of rulership of this herb to Venus.

Pharmacologically, Salvia contains a number of active principles, amongst which are oestrogenlike substances. It also contains vitamins and has antiseptic properties. The presence of oestrogen in the herb means that, like Agnus castus, it can be used as a natural substitute for hormone replacement therapy and is effective against most menopausal symptoms. Its oestrogen content has also led to this herb being traditionally used in the treatment of female infertility. Sage is a herb that has drying properties so caution should be exercised in situations where vaginal dryness accompanies the menopause.

The herb is used as an infusion made from 5–10 g of the leaves, taken twice daily. Alternatively, 2–4 ml of the tincture is taken three times a day. As Sage is to be found in most herb gardens, and can be grown in a pot on the window sill, it is a readily available self-help remedy.

FALSE UNICORN ROOT (HELONIAS)
Chamaelirium luteum

This herb comes from the healing traditions of the North American Indians, who used it as a tonic for the female reproductive system. Its active ingredients are oestrogen precursors, which means it contains substances which, when absorbed into the body, are converted into oestrogens. Like Agnus castus, it has an amphoteric action and tends to regularize hormonal functions.

The usual dosage is 3–9 g of the root prepared as an infusion or tea, or 2–4 ml of the tincture, taken three times a day.

BLACK COHOSH (BLACK SNAKE ROOT, SQUAW ROOT)
Cimicifuga racemosa

This herb also comes to us by way of the North American Indians. It is a powerful relaxant and acts as a normalizer of the female reproductive system. It too contains oestrogens and has a balancing effect on the levels of female sex hormones. It is also effective in the treatment of rheumatic conditions, and it has a mentally relaxing effect. Therefore, it may prove a useful herb where the menopause is complicated by arthritis and muscular pain. It may also be beneficial in cases where anxiety and mental tension accompany the menopause.

Usually one teaspoonful of the dried root is boiled with one cup of water for 10–15 minutes, and this is then drunk three times a day. Alternatively, 2–4 ml of the tincture may be taken three times a day.

BETH ROOT (SQUAW ROOT)
Trillium erectum

This plant was prized by the North American Indians as an aphrodisiac. It contains a natural precursor of the female sex hormones, and it has astringent (drying) properties which make it useful in arresting excessive uterine bleeding which may occur at the time of the menopause. For this purpose, it is often given in combination with Golden Seal (*Hydrastis canadensis*), the root of which contains the alkaloids hydrastine, berberine and canadine. As well as having an astringent effect, Beth Root has a tonic effect on the smooth muscle of the uterus, causing it to contract, thus helping to control bleeding.

A herbalist may well prescribe these two herbs to control excessive uterine bleeding connected with the menopause. However, there is a warning which I must give here and which I cannot emphasize too strongly. *Very irregular or excessive bleeding at the time of the menopause may be a sign of a condition that will need surgical intervention and a gynaecological opinion is essential.* Therefore herbal treatment of excessive bleeding, whether prescribed or otherwise, should never be undertaken without first having a thorough check-up by a qualified gynaecologist. Once a gynaecologist has ruled out the need for surgical intervention then, of course, herbal treatment may be very useful in helping to control the distressing symptom of heavy bleeding. I do not wish to alarm you, as most cases of very heavy bleeding will not require surgery, so there is no need for undue anxiety. However, any woman who has this symptom should approach her family doctor in the first instance with a view to being referred to a gynaecologist.

Other herbs which may be used by a herbalist to treat menopausal problems include St John's Wort (*Hypericum perforatum*). This herb contains glycosides and volatile oils and has a sedative and pain-relieving effect. It is used where irritability and anxiety are associated with the menopause.

Another herb sometimes used in the treatment of menopausal symptoms is Life Root (*Senecio aureus*). This is yet another North American Indian remedy, which acts as a uterine tonic, but the plant contains toxic substances and should only be used under medical supervision.

CONTRA-INDICATIONS

I am aware of no evidence to suggest that any of the herbs, with the possible exception of Life Root, have any adverse effects. However, it would seem reasonable to suppose that women who are unable to take HRT for medical reasons should also avoid herbs which contain oestrogen or its precursors. Thus it would be sensible to apply the lists of relative and absolute contra-indications to HRT (given in the last chapter) to the oestrogen-containing herbs mentioned above. A woman who is unable to take HRT, perhaps because she has had breast cancer, would be well advised to avoid the oestrogen-containing herbs mentioned in this chapter (Agnus castus, Salvia, Black Cohosh and Beth Root).

A woman who needs relief from menopausal symptoms but has a medical history that precludes the use of oestrogen would be better advised to try treatment with Homoeopathy or Chinese medicine.

HOMOEOPATHY

Homoeopathy is an energy-based medicine system which is founded on the principle that like is cured by like. That is to say, in order to cure a disease a substance is given that, in health, would itself produce symptoms similar to the disease being treated. The homoeopathic principle (*Similia similibus curantur* ('Like is cured by like') has been attributed to Hippocrates, the Greek physician regarded as the father of Western medicine.

The homoeopathic principle was rediscovered in the eighteenth century by the German scientist and physician, Samuel Hahnemann (1755–1843). He made the practical observation that the symptoms of intermittent fever (malaria) were the same as the symptoms of an overdose of the medicine Cinchona Bark. Cinchona Bark, which contains the alkaloid quinine, was the treatment for malaria in use at the time. This observation, that a disease was cured by a substance which gave rise to similar symptoms as the disease, led him to experiment with other drugs and substances in common use at the time and compare the symptoms produced by the drugs to those of common diseases. For example, he found that the symptoms of poisoning by Belladonna (Deadly Nightshade) resembled those of scarlet fever. He and his colleagues experimented with a large number of substances and the first homoeopathic remedies were born.

The principle of like treating like is not unknown to conventional medicine. For instance, it is utilized in the principle of vaccination, where a substance which causes a mild form of disease is used to prevent a severe form of a similar disease. It is also used in allergy desensitization whereby a small quantity of a substance which causes an allergic reaction when given in large quantities is used to prevent just such a reaction.

So far so good, but what really caused homoeopathy to part company with the conventional medicine of Hahnemann's time was yet another discovery of his. He found that his remedies retained their potency even when they were diluted to a very extreme degree. He called the process of dilution *potentization*. Potentization is carried out as follows: a concentrated solution of the remedy, for example Belladonna, is taken and then one part of the solution is added to 100 parts of a solvent (usually a water and alcohol mixture). The mixture is then violently shaken. (This is known as *sucussion*.) The resulting solution is known as the *first centesimal potency* and is given the designation 1c. In our example, it would be known as Belladonna 1c.

This process of dilution is repeated a number of times. If it is done six times, it yields the sixth potency (Belladonna 6c), and if it is done thirty times, it yields the thirtieth potency (Belladonna 30c). The process of serial dilution can be carried out using a dilution factor of one part solution to ten of solvent, which gives the *decimal* potencies (written 1x, 6x, 30x, and so on in England and 1D, 6D, 30D in Germany and continental Europe). Likewise, if a factor of one to 1000 parts of solvent is used, it yields the *millecimal* potencies (Belladonna 1m, 2m, 10m, etc.). Hahnemann is believed to have derived the idea of potentization from the writings of the Renaissance physician and alchemist, Paracelsus.

Hahnemann attributed the fact that his remedies retained their effectiveness even in extreme dilutions to the idea that, as the material substance was diluted out of the remedy, so a spiritual force entered into it. Here we can see an interesting analogy between homoeopathy and the menopause, which can be seen as a time when spiritual forces are able to enter the life of a woman as she passes away from activities such as childrearing and caring for a family, which tie her to the material world. Once a remedy has been diluted beyond the twelfth centecimal potency (12c), it can be calculated from the laws of physical chemistry that there is no longer a single molecule of the original substance left in the remedy. Yet anyone who has more than a superficial acquaintance with homoeopathy finds that the remedies are still active. Indeed, the most common potency used by homoeopathic doctors in Britain is the thirtieth centecimal potency (30c), far too dilute to contain any molecules of the original diluted substance. A paper published in the prestigious scientific journal *Nature* in 1988 showed that homoeopathic dilutions of antibodies were still able to bring about changes in cells in tissue culture despite being too dilute to contain any molecules of the original antibody.[4] The furore which followed publication of this paper said more about the scientific establishment, who emerged with no credit, than it did about the accuracy or otherwise of the original research.

Again, a paper published in the British Medical Journal in 1991 showed that the majority of clinical trials conducted into the effectiveness of homoeopathy have shown that it works.[5] So there is no shortage of evidence of the efficacy of homoeopathy, and of extreme dilutions.

An explanation of how the extreme dilutions work may be more mundane than Hahnemann's 'spiritual force'. In order to see how such dilutions can be effective, we need first to consider the molecular structure of water. It is known that ice is a tightly bonded lattice of water molecules. Physical chemistry demonstrates that, when ice melts, it only absorbs 27 per cent of the heat that would be needed to break all of the bonds between molecules in the lattice. In other words, water in its liquid form also exists in the form of joined molecular lattices. The molecules of water are joined together in groups of two, five or more. These groups of molecules are constantly in vibration. In the same way, each individual water molecule, consisting of one oxygen atom and two hydrogen atoms, also vibrates within itself.

Figure 1 shows the different ways in which hydrogen atoms can vibrate in relation to an oxygen atom within a single water molecule. With such complex interactions going on both between and within water molecules, it is easy to see that these vibrations could be influenced by the process of dilution and sucussion of a remedy. Thus the energetic imprint of the remedy could be transferred to the water solvent during the process of potentization. There is some evidence that this may indeed be the case.

It is known that the electromagnetic absorption spectra of different homoeopathic remedies differ one from another, although they are identical from the viewpoint of ordinary chemical analysis that is, they all consist purely of a water/

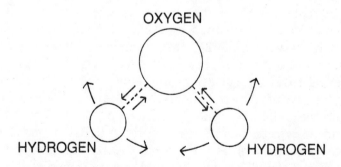

Fig. 1 Hydrogen and oxygen atoms within a single water molecule

alcohol solvent). It has also been demonstrated that homoeopathic remedies emit microwave radiation due to the vibration of the water molecules. Such vibrations and radiations are probably transferred to the patient's own water molecules, bringing about a curative effect.[6]

It is worth recalling here that since the time of Einstein, science has known that matter *is* energy. Science is also aware that fundamental particles, such as electrons, can behave both as particles (matter) and vibration (energy). Therefore, for a scientist in tune with the basis of twentieth-century physics, the idea of a very dilute remedy carrying an energy pattern but no actual matter should not be too hard to deal with. After all, a science which can ascribe 'strangeness numbers' to fundamental particles, numbers which describe the extent to which the particles are 'not there', should find the idea of active infinitesimal dilutions very easy to swallow. The only people who might have trouble accepting these concepts are those who cling to the notions of nineteenth century science with its insistence on an absolute distinction between energy and matter. Unfortunately, this is the view of the majority of the medical profession today.

HOMOEOPATHY AND THE MENOPAUSE

The most important treatment used by homoeopathic physicians for the menopause is the constitutional remedy. Hahnemann observed that many people behave as if they were chronically poisoned by a particular substance. Someone who is very irritable, easily angered, hypersensitive to noise and lights and very impulsive, acts *as if* they were suffering from a form of chronic poisoning by Nux vomica (a type of nut which contains strychnine). Such a person would be called a 'Nux vomica type' and Nux vomica would be said to be his or her constitutional remedy. Likewise, someone who is thin, tired, weepy and pale yet who feels better from exercise would be described as a Sepia type and their constitutional remedy would be Sepia. An untidy, argumentative, introspective type who is fond of eating sweet foods would be described as having the constitutional type corresponding to the remedy Sulphur.

There are a number of such constitutional remedies, all corresponding to a differing physical and mental type. The constitutional remedy is considered to be very deep-acting, and is often used to treat mental problems. It is particularly useful at times when deep-rooted changes are occurring, such as during the menopause. The only way to find out which is your particular constitutional remedy is to consult a homoeopathic practitioner. Deciding on the constitutional remedy requires a detailed knowledge of each remedy, and even if one did possess such knowledge, it would still be very difficult to decide one's own constitutional type as we do not see ourselves objectively.

Besides the constitutional remedy, there are a number of other remedies that a homoeopath might recommend for particular symptoms (although in some cases these may be identical to the constitutional remedy for a given patient).

SEPIA

One of the most commonly used homoeopathic remedies in the menopause, and one which is used for many female complaints, is Sepia. This is made from the ink of the cuttlefish. It is particularly suited to thin women of a sallow appearance who are irritable and weepy and feel 'worn out', often from hard work. It used to be called the 'washer-woman's remedy'. She may have a low backache, a loss of sexual appetite and may be depressed.

Hahnemann first became interested in Sepia when one of his patients, an artist, became ill and emaciated, seemingly for no apparent reason. He observed him and noticed that he licked his brush dipped in Sepia in order to achieve a fine point for painting. The artist was being poisoned by Sepia, yet when it was given in potentized form, he got better. Later on homoeopathic physicians came to use Sepia as a hormonal remedy par excellence. It may also be a useful remedy for depression.

The Sepia patient often feels and acts in a dejected manner, often wishing to escape the burden of family commitments. The Sepia patient feels better for exercise and is often fond of dancing. They tend to perspire easily. Sepia is often given in a high potency (for instance, 10m) at the menopause.

PULSATILLA

Another important remedy used by homoeopaths is Pulsatilla which is particularly effective in cases where the woman is excessively weepy and in need of consolation. This is prepared from the pasque flower or wind flower (*Anemone pulsatilla*) which is also used in western herbalism as a sedative and as a remedy for menstrual pains. Homoeopathically, it is used at the menopause particularly for women who fit the picture of the Pulsatilla type. They are often fair with blue eyes and traditionally have a gentle, yielding disposition. They may well feel better in the open air. The Pulsatilla patient tends to be emotionally labile and is easily moved both to tears and laughter.

Pulsatilla is also often used for leucorrhoea (vaginal discharge) around the time of the menopause. Homoeopaths may also prescribe it for non-specific changes in the cervical smear which can occur at this time. In this case, it is given in a low potency (6c), twice daily. For emotional problems it would be given in a higher potency.

AGNUS CASTUS

A very useful menopausal remedy which we have already encountered in the section on western herbalism. Homoeopathically this is given in the 3x potency twice daily until there is a response. It may be used for a multiplicity of symptoms which accompany the menopause such as loss of memory, despair, anxiety, fear, headaches, flabby muscles, and for cases where many minor non-specific complaints are associated with the menopause.

REMEDIES FOR HOT FLUSHES AND NIGHT SWEATS

For hot flushes and night sweating, homoeopathy has a number of other remedies at its disposal. Salvia (Sage) tincture is often used, as in herbalism. It is especially useful for flushes moving from the chest upwards. It is given in a dose of 7–10 drops at night in water, increasing if necessary to 20 drops.

One advantage of the use of potentized, or diluted, remedies is that extremely toxic substances can be given for their homoeopathic effect without fear of poisoning or unpleasant side effects. One such remedy is Lachesis. This is the venom of the surukuku or bushmaster snake, the most venomous snake on earth, found in parts of the tropics. Suitably diluted, the venom yields a powerful remedy for hot flushes. It is particularly used for cases where there are flushes with palpitations and headache, a feeling of constriction around the throat and sudden rushes of blood to the head. There is sometimes a feeling of choking and the patient may not be able to tolerate anything being worn around the neck. It may also be used for heavy periods around the time of the menopause. It may be given in high potency, for instance 200c.

Two conventional allopathic drugs also yield valuable remedies for hot flushes when given in homoeopathic dilutions. These are Glonoine (glyceryl trinitrate) and Amyl nitrite. Glonoine is used particularly where hot flushes are accompanied by a throbbing in the head. Amyl nitrite is used for hot flushes which come on very suddenly and are accompanied by headaches, anxiety and palpitations.

Sulphur is also used for hot flushes, especially when these occur in the sulphur type of patient who is untidy, introspective, and fond of sweet and fatty foods.

Kali. carb. (potassium carbonate) is given for hot flushes associated with backache and a feeling of weakness in the back and legs. Symptoms are typically worse between 2am and 4am. Kali. carb. is also given for the symptoms of making mistakes in speech, missing words out, putting wrong ones in, or being unable to remember the word one wishes to use. This is a symptom often associated with the menopause.

Aurum metallicum (metallic gold) is given for hot flushes associated with melancholia and even thoughts of suicide. It would be given in potencies of 30c and above.

Graphites can be used for flushing, particularly where it affects the face. There is often a tendency to put on weight and nosebleeds may occur.

Belladonna is given for hot flushes affecting the head and face associated with redness, congestion and sweating of the face.

Calcarea carbonica (calcium carbonate from crushed oyster shells) is also used for hot flushes to the head accompanied by sweating of the head. It is a watery remedy and is also given for women who are overweight at the time of the menopause due to water retention. The Calc. carb. patient tends to be pale with a tendency towards flabbiness. They feel the cold easily. For water retention, Calc. carb. may be given in high potency (eg. 200c) once a week until the condition has improved.

OTHER REMEDIES

There are a number of other homoeopathic remedies which may prove useful around the time of the menopause. Osteo-arthritis and osteoporosis occurring at this time may respond to Sepia.

Where they fit the constitutional picture, the remedies Nat. mur. (Natrum muriaticum or Sodium chloride) and Nux vomica may be of use in treating menopausal symp-toms. Nat. mur. patients are reticent and nervous, which they sometimes cover up with a self-assured appearance. They like salty food and their symptoms are worse from heat. Nux vomica patients are anxious, irritable, easily ang-ered and with a fiery temperament. They are fastidious and may have difficulty sleeping. They may overindulge in food and drink. They correspond well to the stereotype of the hard-pressed, high-flying executive, whether male or female.

Where menopausal symptoms are accompanied by great feelings of resentment, the remedy Staphisagria may prove useful.

For heavy bleeding around the time of the menopause, Sepia and Pulsatilla may prove useful, especially where these are the constitutional remedy. Phosphorus is also used for excessive bleeding, especially in women who have a tendency to bleed easily.

Yet another remedy which may be of value in the menopause is Murex. This is prepared from a sea mollusc and resembles Sepia. The Murex patient is sometimes described as a 'sexy Sepia'. It is particularly useful for cases where the menopause is complicated by Pre-Menstrual Syndrome (PMS) with soreness of the breasts and water retention. A suitable regime would be the 6c potency given twice daily until improvement occurs.

Where menopausal symptoms are associated with a feeling of vaginal prolapse and a sensation of pressing down in the bladder, vagina and rectum, Lilium tigrium (the Tiger Lily) can be prescribed.

Some other useful remedies are Bryonia for dryness of the vagina and thinning of its walls, and Ignatia for globus hystericus, a sensation of having a lump in the throat. The patient's constitutional remedy would also be useful for these conditions.

The above is by no means an exhaustive list. A good homoeopath always matches the remedy to the patient, and so when you consult a homoeopath he or she may decide that some other remedy is called for apart from the ones mentioned here. This is because homoeopathy is aimed at treating the patient in her entirety, rather than just suppressing symptoms as conventional allopathic medicine tends to do.

CHINESE MEDICINE

Chinese medicine is one of the three surviving systems of traditional medicine which have come down to us from the ancient world. (The other two are the Ayurvedic system of India, and Tibetan medicine.) It is at least 5000 years old, the discovery of Chinese herbal medicine being attributed to the legendary emperor, Shen Nong (3493 BC).

The concepts of Chinese medicine may at first seem strange to the westerner, particularly to those with a training in western science and physiology. However, it is a logically self-consistent system, and within its own framework is able to provide an explanation for many of the puzzling symptoms which accompany the menopause, for instance hot flushes, which western medicine is unable to account for fully within its present knowledge.

Chinese medicine also has some fascinating philosophical ideas concerning the nature of the menopause, which every woman who is at this stage of life should find relevant and interesting. Unfortunately, these cannot be understood without some knowledge of the concepts underlying Chinese medicine and physiology. We will, therefore, briefly examine these concepts before looking at the practical uses of Chinese medicine in the menopause. In a book such as this, our look at the philosophical concepts must necessarily be an over-simplification, as entire volumes can be written on just this one subject. However, even a brief examination will give a better understanding of what this system of medicine has to offer.

THE PHILOSOPHY OF CHINESE MEDICINE

Yin and yang

A fundamental concept in Chinese medicine is that of **yin** and **yang**. According to the Chinese, present throughout the universe on all levels are two energies known as yin and yang, which are opposites yet complementary. Yin is dark, cold, feminine in nature, heavy and still. Yang is light, hot, masculine in nature, light in weight and mobile. The presence of yin and yang is easy to see all around us, in the cycles of day and night, winter and summer, and so on. In the body a fever would be yang and hypothermia yin. A state of bodily overactivity is yang and underactivity is yin.

On a more mundane level, the Chinese see oil as a yin substance, thus the oil in a motor car acts as yin to counteract the heating nature of the fuel (yang). Without oil (yin) the car's bearings would overheat and seize up and the car would not go at all. So, for effective functioning of anything, no matter what, yin and yang need to be balanced and in harmony. On a global level, modern man extracts oil (yin) from the earth. This causes a deficiency of yin in the earth, leaving a relative excess of yang. The earth then becomes too yang (or hot) and global warming results.

On the level of the individual human being, we are all born with a fixed quantity of yin and yang. Yin, being the most delicate, is used up first. According to the Chinese, we have used up half of our supply of yin by the age of forty. There is therefore a tendency for the body to become yin-deficient as it ages. Much of Chinese medicine is aimed at restoring the balance between yin and yang when this becomes disturbed and leads to disease.

Qi

Another concept central to Chinese medicine is that of **Qi** (or Chi, as it used to be written). This is perhaps best translated as 'vital energy'. There are a number of different sorts of Qi in the body, each of which has a particular function. Qi circulates between the different organs and it also circulates near the surface of the body in special channels called acupuncture meridians (or *Jing-luo* in Chinese). These channels connect up with the organs in the interior of the body.

According to the Chinese, for the body to be in health, there must be adequate amounts of Qi and it must be able to flow freely, or disease results. The basis of the science of acupuncture is to promote the free flow of Qi in the meridians by inserting fine needles at specific points on those meridians.

Blood (Xue)

The Chinese also have a concept of **Blood** *(Xue)*. This differs from the western view in that Blood is regarded as having an energetic component as well as a material one. Blood is related to yin, and is regarded as yin in relation to Qi. Qi is regarded as yang in relation to Blood.

Jing

Another Chinese concept which is vital to the understanding of the menopause is that of **Jing**. It is perhaps best translated as 'primal essence'. We are all born with a certain complement of Jing, which we acquire from our parents. This is known as pre-natal Jing and most authorities say that it cannot be added during life. Once all this Jing has been used up, then death ensues.

The Chinese see the outward physical manifestation of Jing as menstrual blood in the female and semen (or sperm) in the male. Consequently, every time a woman menstruates, a small amount of Jing is lost, which cannot be replaced. Blood too has an energetic component, as we have seen. This concept leads Honora Lee Wolfe, in her excellent book *Second Spring*,[7] to make the interesting observation that in Chinese terms, the menopause can be seen as a *'natural mechanism to slow down the ageing process in women'*. Thus, the cessation of periods at the menopause leads to a decreased loss of Jing, postponing its eventual exhaustion which coincides with the end of life.

The five elements

We have looked so far at the concepts of yin and yang, Qi (vital energy), Blood and Jing (primal essence). There is one more concept we need to grasp before we can understand how Chinese medicine views the menopause. This is the concept of the Five Elements. Chinese medicine, in common with the Ayurvedic and Tibetan systems, considers the human body, like the universe, to be made up of five elements or energies. In Chinese medicine, these elements are given the names Metal, Water, Wood, Fire and Earth (these are symbolic names only and do not represent the actual substances metal, wood, etc.).

Associated with each element are particular bodily organs. The elements and the five main solid organs associated with each one are shown in Figure 2.

Chinese medicine recognizes the importance of five main organs: the lungs, the kidney, the liver, the heart and the spleen. The Chinese concept of the function of these organs

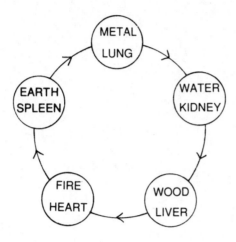

Fig. 2 The Five Elements, the five solid organs, and the cycle of supply of energy, or *Sheng* cycle

is not exactly the same as the western view, however. For example, under the function of the kidney, the Chinese also include those functions which in the west are ascribed to the sex glands and the adrenal glands (which are situated on top of the kidneys).

If you look again at Figure 2, you will see that a circle links the five organs. This shows the cycle of transmission of energy (or Qi) between the five organs (or Sheng cycle, as it is called in Chinese). The lung supplies energy to the kidney, the kidney supplies it to the liver, the liver supplies the heart, the heart supplies the spleen, and the spleen supplies the lung. In addition to this cycle of energy supply, there is another cycle in which each organ acts as a controlling influence on the organ two places on in the circle. This controlling (or K'o cycle) is represented by the dotted lines in Figure 3 (page 58).

So, the energy of the lung regulates the energy of the liver and prevents it becoming excessive. Similarly the liver controls the spleen, the spleen controls the kidney, the kidney controls the heart, and the heart controls the lung. It can be seen, therefore, that if one of the organs is

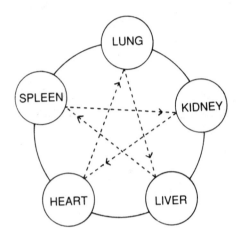

Fig. 3   The *K'o* or controlling cycle

disturbed, the function of one or more of the other organs is likely to be affected as well.

THE MENOPAUSE IN CHINESE MEDICINE

Unlike western medicine, which views every woman's menopause as the same and always prescribes the same treatment for it, namely HRT, Chinese medicine recognizes a number of different energetic disturbances which can occur during the menopause, each one of which has different symptoms and is treated in a different way. Like homoeopathic medicine, Chinese medicine tailors its therapies to the individual patient rather than the disease or condition from which they suffer, as western medicine tends to do. The most important and common energetic disturbance which occurs at the time of the menopause is kidney yin deficiency.

Kidney yin deficiency

According to the Chinese, the primary event at the menopause is a deficiency of kidney yin. We have earlier seen that yin is feminine and that the Chinese also regard the ovaries as part of what they refer to as the 'kidney', So, kidney yin deficiency tallies with the western definition of the menopause as primary ovarian failure when the ovaries cease to produce female sex hormones. However, it is perhaps unwise to draw too many parallels between very different systems of medicine.

The great Chinese medical classic *The Nei Ching* or *Yellow Emperor's Classic of Internal Medicine*,[8] states that the life of woman is governed by a series of seven-year cycles. At age 7, the energy of the kidneys becomes abundant, her teeth become strong and her hair grows long. At age 14 (2 × 7), she begins to menstruate and her energy is strong. At age 21, she is fully grown, all her teeth are present and the energy of the kidneys is steady. Finally at age 49 (7 × 7), the kidney energy declines and menstruation ceases. As already mentioned, there is a general tendency for the body to become yin-deficient as it grows older. So, a natural state of kidney yin deficiency is arrived at around the time of the forty ninth year. We have seen from the diagram of the Sheng cycle that the kidney transmits energy to the liver. So, if the kidney is deficient in yin, then the liver becomes yin-deficient as well (see Figure 4 overleaf).

Therefore, what is more commonly seen in practice is a combined picture of both kidney yin deficiency and liver yin deficiency rather than the pure kidney yin deficiency.

Kidney yin and liver yin deficiency

The deficiency of yin in the kidney and the liver leads to a relative excess of yang. As we have seen, yang energy is hot and mobile and has a tendency to rise upwards as it is light in nature. This gives a clinical picture of heat rising upwards. The result is hot flushes and sweating, especially in the upper part of the body.

As the liver rules the eyes according to Chinese medicine, there may occur blurred vision, spots in front of the eyes, and dizziness. Headaches and tinnitus may also occur. The lower back is the 'palace of the kidneys' according to the Chinese, and the lack of kidney energy there may lead to low backache or pain in the legs. The deficiency of yin (or

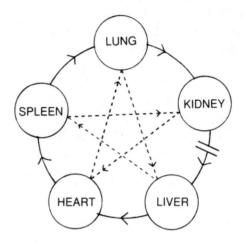

Fig. 4   The kidney fails to transmit energy to the liver, so both are yin-deficient

fluid) may give a dry mouth and throat, and constipation may also result. Insomnia and dream-disturbed sleep may also occur.

Liver yang rising

If the yin deficiency is particularly severe, there may be a large relative excess of yang in the liver, which then tends to flow upwards. This particularly occurs if liver Qi stagnation is present (see below).

The clinical picture of liver yang rising is like a more severe form of kidney and liver yin deficiency. As well as the hot flushes and sweats due to rising yang there may occur dizziness and vertigo, tinnitus and red eyes, migraines, a bitter taste in the mouth, irritability or loss of temper, and profuse menstrual flow. The Chinese say that anger is an emotion associated with the liver, so the excessive liver yang may cause irritability and sudden outbursts of anger. The excess yang (heat) causes the blood to become overheated, leading to heavy menstrual flow.

Liver Qi stagnation

This is a situation which may complicate the bio-energetic state at the time of the menopause. As mentioned above, anger is an emotion associated with the liver. According to Chinese medical theory, an excessive amount of anger can damage the Qi of the liver, causing it to stagnate. Honora Lee Wolfe points out that menopausal and post-menopausal women have ample reason to be angry and frustrated as we live in a society in which older women are not valued and have no clearly defined social role. This, combined with the general high level of stress present in urban society, means that liver Qi stagnation is fairly common at the time of the menopause and may complicate other bio-energetic patterns which occur. Liver Qi stagnation may lead to distension and bloating, a feeling of oppression at the sides of the chest, and emotional lability. It may also predispose to the syndrome of liver yang rising.

Stagnant liver Qi can give rise also to a syndrome of liver fire. This can result in painful breasts, depression, anger and irritability. The painful breasts are due to the fact that the liver acupuncture meridian runs on the front of the chest. This pattern clearly resembles that of pre-menstrual syndrome (PMS) which can be seen as a transient form of Liver Qi stagnation.

Kidney yang deficiency

We have seen that kidney yin deficiency, the primary event in the menopause, gives rise to an excess of kidney yang. However, this excess of yang is only relative; in actual fact, if yin is depleted, yang is always depleted as well, though usually to a lesser extent. However, it may happen that the kidney yang energy is more depleted than usual and signs of kidney yang deficiency appear.

We have seen that yang is a hot energy, therefore yang deficiency manifests as signs of cold. This may give rise to a feeling of cold in the body and limbs, and an aversion to cold. The complexion is often pale, and pain and a feeling of coldness may be present in the lower back. There may be a lack of energy, and lack of kidney yang may manifest as an absent or low sex drive. There may be also copious clear urine or fluid retention.

Kidney yang deficiency may be complicated by spleen yang deficiency, in which case there is a tendency to greater fluid retention, obesity, abdominal distension and loose stools.

Kidney yin and yang deficiency

Both kidney yin and yang may be deficient, in which case a clinical picture having features of both may arise. Signs of both heat and cold are present and there may be a feeling of coldness of the limbs and especially the lower body while at the same time there are hot flushes of the head, neck and face. There may be dizziness, sweating of the palms, tiredness and a low sex drive.

Kidneys and heart not communicating

We saw from our look at the K'o cycle that the kidneys (Water element) usually exert a controlling action on the heart (Fire element). However, if the kidneys are lacking in energy, they will be unable to control the heart properly. The heart then becomes overactive (see Figure 5).

Thus in Five Element terms, Water fails to control Fire and the Fire blazes out of control. Fire blazes up while the Water trickles down.

The heart is said to control the mind in Chinese medicine. Therefore, when the heart is overactive, mental symptoms such as insomnia, nervousness and anxiety, palpitations and dream-disturbed sleep will appear. The downward movement of the Water element may result in vaginal discharge, incontinence or dribbling urination, and uterine bleeding.

Heart yin deficiency and heart blood deficiency

A similar lack of communication between kidney and heart can lead to heart yin deficiency or heart blood deficiency. If heart blood deficiency predominates, the symptoms will mainly be mental, with dream-disturbed sleep, palpitations, loss of memory and insomnia.

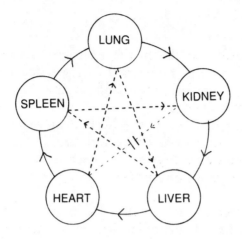

Fig. 5   Kidney failing to control heart

If heart yin deficiency predominates, the symptoms are those of heat in the soles of the feet, palms of the hands and centre of the chest, restlessness and night sweats. A low-grade fever can occur in the afternoon.

The above review of Chinese medicine is necessarily a simplification, and those who wish to examine such topics in greater depth are referred to Honora Lee Wolfe's excellent text *Second Spring*.

TREATMENT OF MENOPAUSAL SYMPTOMS BY CHINESE MEDICINE

Chinese medicine has a number of therapeutic methods at its disposal; these include therapeutic exercises and breathing techniques (*Qi-gong*), dietetics, acupuncture and herbalism. We shall consider here Chinese herbalism and acupuncture/acupressure.

CHINESE HERBALISM

Yin tonics

We have seen that the prime energetic disturbance of the menopause is yin deficiency, in particular kidney yin deficiency. Therefore the Chinese use herbs which will tonify the yin energy.

The main yin tonic is the herb *Rehmannia glutinosa* (Shu Di Huang). The roots of this herb are dark and sticky, and have a pleasant sweet taste. The herb is also used in Chinese cookery and can sometimes be bought in Chinese supermarkets.

Chinese herbs are usually given in combination with other herbs to enhance their action and also to remove any possible side effects. Rehmannia is usually given in the form of **Liu Wei Di Huang Wan** (Rehmannia Six formula), yin tonic pills consisting of Rehmannia with the addition of six other herbs. The whole prescription has been shown experimentally to have the effect of normalizing the body, reducing excitement of the nervous system, regulating hormone function, lowering blood sugar and blood pressure, and improving the function of the kidney.

The addition of two sedative herbs to this prescription gives 'Eight Flavour Tea' or **Zhi Bai Ba Wei Wan**, one of the most commonly used Chinese remedies for menopausal symptoms.

Where yin deficiency leads to liver yang rising, with hot flushes to the head, headaches, dizziness and irritability, **Qi Ju Di Huang Wan** (Chrysanthemum and Lycii) pills are used. These are the basic yin tonic formula with the addition of two herbs to reduce yang and nourish the liver. For acute hot flushes and severe night sweats, **Da Bu Yin Wan** is used. This is a strong yin tonic formula consisting of Rehmannia and three other herbs.

For liver Qi stagnation, **Xiao Yao Wan** is used. These pills contain the herb Chai Hu (Bupleureum or Hare's Ear) which is the main liver herb in Chinese medicine. They are used where the menopause is complicated by anger, irritability, bad temper, and sore breasts, and are also a good remedy for PMS.

When the clinical picture is one of kidney yang deficiency, with coldness, lack of energy and a reduced sex drive, then **You Gui Wan** is used. This consists of Rehmannia plus several herbs which tonify the yang energy, such as *Cuscuta japonica* or Dodder.

Where a clinical picture of 'heart and kidney not communicating' arises, with nervousness, anxiety, palpitations, insomnia and dream-disturbed sleep, **Tien Wan Pu Hsin Tang** or Emperor Tea is called for. This prescription, which is available in pill form, is an ancient remedy for nourishing the *Shen*, or spirit, and it comes from the mystical Taoist tradition of Chinese philosophy. Its main ingredient is again Rehmannia with the addition of a number of other herbs to nourish heart yin and heart Blood, so relieving nervousness, insomnia and palpitations.

When the spleen energies are disturbed, then **Gui Pi Tang** may be used. This prescription soothes the nerves and nourishes the heart as well as invigorating the spleen. It contains Ginseng as well as Dang Gui (Chinese Angelica). This latter herb is sometimes called 'Woman's Ginseng' and is the main herb used in Chinese medicine for disturbances of menstruation. **Gui Pi Tang** is particularly useful if very heavy periods occur during the menopause.

Most of the remedies mentioned above are available in pill form and are inexpensive. They can easily be obtained in all western countries, but they should only be taken on the advice of someone trained in Chinese medicine as, if the wrong remedy is taken, the situation may be made worse. For instance, if a yang tonic is taken when a yin tonic is required, the imbalance between yin and yang will be exaggerated and the situation may deteriorate instead of getting better. Therefore, it is essential to consult a practitioner who has been trained in making the correct Chinese diagnosis and who will know which remedy to prescribe.

Besides the remedies mentioned above for treating menopausal syndrome, there are some other remedies used by the Chinese to deal with conditions which can occur at or around the menopause. For excessive menstrual bleeding, the patent medicine **Yunnan Bai Yao** can be used. This is a most interesting remedy. It consists of a powder, and its

exact formula is a Chinese state secret. It is known, however, that its main active ingredient is a type of Ginseng
called Panax Notoginseng. Notoginseng has the unusual
property of being able both to stop bleeding and to dissolve
blood-clots depending on which is required.

As I said earlier, herbal treatment for excessive menstrual
bleeding should only be undertaken after a gynaecologist's
opinion has been obtained.

Osteoporosis

The Chinese have a number of remedies for the prevention
and treatment of osteoporosis, the most useful of which is
the herb **He Shou Wu** (*Polygonum multifolium* or Chinese
Cornbind). Like the better known Ginseng, this herb
entered Chinese medicine by way of the esoteric Taoist
school of philosophy. It tonifies the energy of the liver and
kidney, and is also said to nourish Blood and Jing.

He Shou Wu also has the property of lowering blood
cholesterol levels. The Chinese also attribute to it the
properties of returning colour to grey hair, and of preserv-
ing a youthful countenance. (The name He Shou Wu means
'black-haired mister' in Chinese.) Whether or not it really
does possess these last two properties, there is no doubt
that it is an excellent tonic for those in the second half of
life. In the opinion of the writer, this herb deserves to be
as well known in the west as is Ginseng. As it is a tonic
herb, it needs to be taken over an extended period of time.
It is best taken together with a yin tonic, such as Rehmannia
glutinosa. A suitable dose would be 10g of both herbs daily,
or a desertspoonful of the tincture of both herbs twice daily.
The herbs are usually given over a course of three months,
which is repeated with intervals of two to three months
between treatment. These herbs too, are best taken under
the supervision of someone trained in Chinese medicine,
particularly as a practitioner may add other herbs to suit
the individual patient's needs.

Another Chinese herb used to treat and prevent osteoporosis is **Wu Jia Pi** (*Eleutherococcus* or Siberian Ginseng).
Like He Shou Wu, this herb also nourishes the liver and
kidneys. It also has an antirheumatic action, and has

antistress and antifatigue properties. It can normalize blood sugar levels, stimulate the immune system, and is a good general tonic. Its activities have been extensively researched by the Russians, who give it to their astronauts.

ACUPUNCTURE

It was mentioned earlier that the Chinese envisage the vital energy or Qi as flowing in channels or meridians near the surface of the body. When imbalances in this energy occur, they are corrected by inserting fine needles into specific points on these channels. This allows the Qi to flow freely, the body's energies are rebalanced and symptoms are relieved.

Acupuncture can be as effective in relieving menopausal symptoms as it is in many other conditions. It is particularly effective at relieving symptoms of pain. It also has a marked relaxing effect, so it would be particularly useful where the menopause is complicated by headaches, anxiety and insomnia. Research has established that acupuncture raises the levels of certain chemicals, known as endorphins, in the brain and peripheral nervous system. The name *endorphin* is short for endogenous morphine and, as this name implies, its action resembles that of the opiate group of painkillers. So, endorphins act as the body's own natural painkiller and sedative. This explains why acupuncture can be effective against pain, why it can have a sedative action, and why some people experience a feeling of well-being after acupuncture treatment.

It has also been found that acupuncture points have different electrical properties from the rest of the skin. They have a lower electrical resistance and there are acupuncture point detectors available which work on this principle. It may be that acupuncture therapy also has an electrical basis, and a direct-current system in the body responsible for repair and regeneration has been postulated.[9]

Those women who wish to have acupuncture treatment should ensure that they only consult a qualified, registered and sympathetic practitioner.

ACUPRESSURE

For those who dislike needles, or for those situations where acupuncture is impractical (for instance, when a hot flush comes on while commuting to work on the train), acupressure is a self-help therapy which may be of benefit. Although definitely less effective than acupuncture, it may still be very useful. Acupressure involves stimulating an acupuncture point with one's finger or thumb rather than with a needle.

The most effective way to stimulate a point is by using what the Chinese call 'one-finger meditation'. This involves pressing on the point with the thumb or forefinger and massaging with a circular motion thirty times. Do not press too hard or the point may become sore. Those acupuncture points which are likely to be of benefit in the menopause are shown in Figures 6, 7 and 8.

All points shown are present bilaterally; that is, they are present on both sides of the body and should be stimulated on both sides. The function of the points illustrated is as follows:

Kidney 1 (K1)	Tonifies yin and subdues heat
Kidney 3 (K3)	Tonifies the Qi of the kidneys
Kidney 6 (K6)	Tonifies kidney yin
Kidney 7 (K7)	Tonifies kidney yang
Kidney 9 (K9)	Tonifies kidney yin and calms the mind
Spleen 6 (Sp6)	Strengthens kidneys and spleen; acts on the uterus and menstruation; regulates hormone balance. Should not be used during pregnancy
Liver 3 (Liv3)	Smooths the flow of liver Qi; calms the mind; stops headaches
Stomach 36 (St36)	Tonifies Qi and calms the mind
Heart 7 (H7)	Calms the heart and the mind
Heart 6 (H6)	Nourishes heart yin and calms the mind; stops sweating
Large intestine 4 (Li4)	Removes heat and stops sweating
Large intestine 11 (Li11)	Clears heat and cools blood
Small intestine 3 (Si3)	Stops sweating

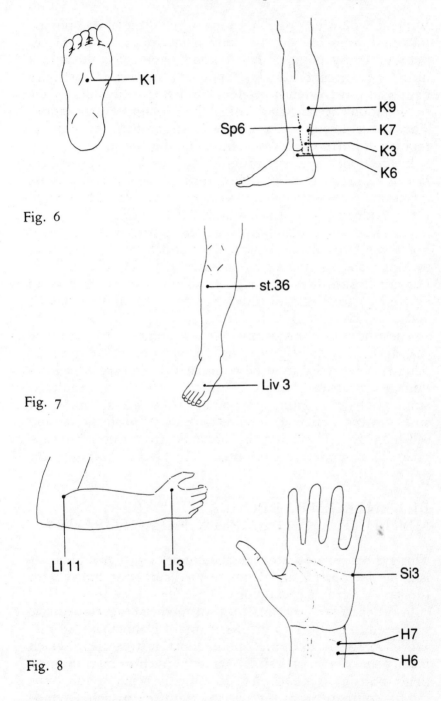

Fig. 6

Fig. 7

Fig. 8

Fig. 6–8 Acupuncture points for menopausal symptoms

While it would be possible to massage all the above points, it would probably not be convenient for most people to massage every point daily. A good regime for those in a hurry is to massage K1, K3, Sp6, St36 and H7 at least once daily and more often if desired. Points on both sides of the body should be massaged using the one-finger meditation. The above group of points will strengthen the kidney, regularize hormone levels, and calm the mind.

In addition, the lower abdomen below the navel (or *Dantien* in Chinese) can be rubbed thirty times in a clockwise direction. The waist and lower back can also be rubbed. Other kidney points can be added if desired.

For headaches, irritability and insomnia, massage Liv3. For loss of sex drive, massage K7 and Sp6. For excessive sweating and night sweats, massage K7, H6, Li4 and Si3. For hot flushes use Li4 and Li11. These can be used as an emergency treatment during a hot flush. K7 and H6 can be added as well.

The above are just some of the points which can be massaged as a self-help 'first aid' for menopausal symptoms. Alternatively, they may be stimulated by means of a low-voltage electrical device designed for the needleless stimulation of acupuncture points. There are a number of such devices available, intended for both professional and self-help use. They may be obtained from specialist suppliers of acupuncture equipment (see Useful Addresses).

BIO-ENERGETIC REGULATORY (BER) MEDICINE AND COMPLEX HOMOEOPATHY

This system incorporates therapeutic principles from herbalism, homoeopathy and Chinese medicine, combined with modern electronic technology.

In order to see how this form of medicine developed, we first need to go back to the Germany of Hahnemann's time. We have so far examined homoeopathic treatment which mainly makes use of a single remedy given in high dilution (high potency), the choice of remedy being made by a careful comparison of the remedy with the patient's symptoms and personality. This was the sort of homoeopathy which Hahnemann originally practised, and it is the type which is still most widely practised in the UK, the USA and India. This form of homoeopathy is sometimes called 'classical homoeopathy.'

However, towards the end of his life, Hahnemann himself sometimes administered more than one remedy at a time, and at times used herbal remedies as well. This trend was developed by a group of his followers who developed 'complex remedies' consisting of a number of homoeopathic remedies combined, usually in low potency, and often mixed with a herbal remedy. This type of homoeopathy is known as 'complex homoeopathy' and is the sort most commonly practised in Germany and continental Europe.

Remedies are made up in order to act on particular organs or systems of the body and so can be prescribed, rather like conventional drugs, according to the site of the disease rather than being matched up to the total picture of the patient's symptoms. The classical homoeopath objects that this is a less holistic system as it does not take the patient's whole symptomatology into account. The complex homoeopaths point out that while classical homoeopathy may have worked well in Hahnemann's time, today it is becoming increasingly difficult, as we are all exposed to a greatly increased toxic load in the form of industrial pollution, food additives, smoking, drinking, recreational and medicinal drugs, and pesticide residues. Complex homoeopaths maintain that toxins in the body interfere with the working of classical homoeopathic remedies, so they tend to administer a number of remedies, often herbal, in order to cleanse and detoxify the system so that homoeopathy has a chance to work.

Complex homoeopathy is often associated with a form of diagnosis known as Bio-energetic Regulatory (or BER) Medicine. In the 1970s, a German doctor named Reinhardt Voll developed a system of electrical measurement of acupuncture points. Legend has it that at one of his seminars to demonstrate his system, he was testing a member of the audience and had just diagnosed a prostate problem. The seminar then adjourned for a coffee break. During the interval a doctor present in the audience handed the 'patient' some Populus, a homoeopathic remedy for prostatism which he put in his pocket. When the seminar resumed, Voll continued to test the 'patient' but now could find no trace of the prostatic problem with his electrical equipment, simply due to the fact that the patient had a homoeopathic remedy in his pocket!

This led to the discovery that the introduction of the correct homoeopathic remedy into Voll's electrical apparatus caused a normalization of the abnormal electrical readings and so it could be used to diagnose the remedy needed to correct a disorder. This is the basis of BER medicine. There are two main forms in use at the moment: Electro-Acupuncture according to Voll (EAV) which uses a machine known as the Dermatron or Biotron, and a simpler form which uses a machine known as a Vega Test.

The Vega Test measures the electrical impedance across an acupuncture meridian. When an abnormal reading occurs, various complex homoeopathic remedies are introduced in turn into the circuit until one is found which corrects the electrical reading back to normal. This is the remedy the patient requires. This is a most useful diagnostic system and, at the same time, a powerful demonstration that homoeopathic remedies have measurable physiological effects.

There are a number of complex homoeopathic remedies which are suitable for use in the menopause. The remedies are all made in Germany and are consequently licensed for use throughout the EEC. Amongst such complex remedies are Vicordin Elixir, which contains a number of tonic herbs, and Oophorinum Complex which contains a number of homoeopathic remedies in combination, including some we have looked at already such as Lilium tigrium, Pulsatilla, Murex, Belladonna and Ignatia. Dosage of this latter remedy is 5–40 drops daily.

For hot flushes, a remedy such as Sanguinaria similiaplexe can be used. This consists of a number of homoeopathic remedies in low potency, including Glonoine, Belladonna, Lachesis, Sepia and Arnica. Dosage is 15 drops daily.

A remedy such as Hocura-Femin may be given as a tonic at this time. It contains the herb Agnus castus together with low potency homoeopathic dilutions of Helonias (False Unicorn Root), Black Cohosh, Hydrastis, and Senecio (Life

Root), together with Pulsatilla, Ignatia and Sepia. The dose of this medicine is one teaspoonful 3 times daily.

All the above mentioned remedies are manufactured by the Pascoe Pharmacy of Giessen, Germany.

Although BER medicine has become associated with complex homoeopathy, it does not have to be so. BER electro-diagnostic machines can also be used to prescribe classical homoeopathic remedies as well as herbs, both Chinese and western. They may also be used to choose allopathic remedies, and may help to diagnose and prescribe for treatment of vitamin and mineral deficiencies. Using BER medicine, a skilled practitioner can quickly work out whether a vitamin or mineral deficiency is present and what should be prescribed to correct it. This gives more satisfactory results that blindly taking vitamins and minerals in the hope that they will cure a presumed deficiency.

So, it can be seen that BER medicine has wide applications, not least at the time of the menopause. Those general readers who wish to look into this subject in more depth are recommended to read *21st Century Medicine* by J. N. Kenyon, MD.[10] Health professionals and those with technical knowledge are recommended to the same author's *Modern Techniques of Acupuncture, Vol III*.[11]

SUMMARY

1. *Western Herbalism* uses a number of herbs to treat menopausal symptoms. They nearly all contain oestrogens (female hormones) or its precursors. Agnus castus is one of the principal herbs used.

2. *Classical Homoeopathy* uses the energetic effect of very dilute potentized solutions to achieve a cure. The remedy is matched to the patient's symptoms and personality type. Sepia and Pulsatilla are commonly used menopausal remedies. A number of different remedies, such as Lachesis, are used for hot flushes.

3. *Chinese Medicine* sees the menopause as primarily a state of kidney yin deficiency. A number of herbal remedies are used to treat menopausal symptoms, most based around

the yin tonic herb *Rehmannia glutinosa*. For osteoporosis, the herbs He Shou Wu (*Polygonum multifolium*) and Wu Jia Pi (*Eleutherococcus*, Siberian Ginseng) are used.

Acupuncture and acupressure may also give relief from menopausal symptoms.

4. *Complex Homoeopathy* makes use of mixtures of herbs and low potency homoeopathic remedies. Choice of remedy is usually carried out by means of bio-electronic measurements.

3. ❉ The Menopause Journal

If the menopause is to become an integrated part of life rather than the separate crisis it now is, women must define and share their own experience.[1]

Paula Weideger

KEEPING A JOURNAL

If you are experiencing problems then the best way to reassure yourself (and anyone else who might need convincing) that the physical and emotional discomfort of the menopause is all too real is to keep a written record. The easiest way to make a menopause journal is to photocopy, appropriately enlarged, the pages overleaf and keep them in a looseleaf folder. Those with access to a computer can quickly create a diary file using the same headings.

The day-to-day journal should be in simple note form with all the relevant information for a week, or even for a month, displayed so that the pattern becomes obvious at a glance. Journal entries can be jotted down at odd moments but many women like to have a special time devoted to recording the intimate detail of their life to honour what is happening in their bodies. Entries should, certainly during the initial period, be made on a regular basis and completed each night before going to bed and then again in the morning to add the events of the night.

The menopause journal is, however, the ideal place to record *everything* about your menopause. This means that the exercises and visualizations included in this book can be written up as looseleaf sheets which are then placed in the folder. As the journal can be kept totally confidential, you will then have an invaluable source of information on exactly what is going on in your life, the patterns you have recognized, how you are changing and developing, and the insights that you gain.

SUGGESTED JOURNAL LAYOUT

DATE	Mon	Tues	Wed
DAY OF CYCLE			
MOON PHASE			
MOOD/EMOTIONS			
SITUATION			
SYMPTOMS			
SLEEP			
DREAMS			
FOOD			
TREATMENTS			

Thurs	Fri	Sat	Sun

It is important to remember to date all the looseleaf entries so that they can be quickly linked to the appropriate day, and the page number of the entry should be cross-referenced onto the daily entries to facilitate finding it again when required. There is nothing more frustrating, or offputting, than having to wade through pages of entries to search for a vital clue, so it is well worth spending a few moments on ensuring easy access.

If any further amplification is required for entries in the day-to-day journal, such as 'dreams', 'situation' or 'mood', this can be included in the expanded journal. Fully recording changes of mood, fluctuating feelings and otherwise incomprehensible emotions is one of the best ways of clarifying what is really happening, as well as providing a valuable release for feelings which could otherwise be bottled up, to explode at a more volatile moment. Once the therapeutic value of the expanded journal has been established, you may well find that it becomes a valued daily ritual during which you record all your inner feelings, traumas and insights. For most people, this is therapy enough but for some it can be the key to realization that some counselling, or joining a self-help group or workshop, would be helpful at this time, particularly if it becomes clear that issues from the past (especially any type of physical or emotional abuse) are still having an effect on the present.

Each of the entry headings is relevant to your total experience and the journal will enable you to make important connections between moods, stressful situations, certain foods and physical symptoms, such as the possible link between coffee and hot flushes, as well as allowing an exploration of feelings you may have been unaware of, possibly for years.

JOURNAL ENTRIES

DAY OF CYCLE

Entering the day of the cycle at the top quickly enables you to see the variations in the pattern of your periods and ties fluctuations of mood, libido, etc., and obscure symptoms such as backache, to specific parts of the men-strual cycle.

It is common during the early menopause for the duration of the cycle to either lengthen or shorten, or for the flow to become lighter or heavier, and some departure from your own particular 'normal' pattern is to be expected. However, it can be useful to fill in days of actual bleeding with a red pen (perhaps using a variation of strokes to indicate a heavy or light flow) so that these stand out, enabling you to identify any 'abnormal' bleeding which may need medical advice. Prolonged or frequent bleeding, which may well cause tiredness or anaemia, can also be identified quickly and appropriate action taken.

This entry will one day signal the welcome news that the menopause is completed.

MOON PHASE

Since reading *The Wise Wound*,[2] and particularly since living in the country where the light pollution is much less and so the light of the full Moon is an inescapable fact of life, I have been aware of how the phases of the Moon link into menstruation.

The post-hysterectomy woman and the menopausal woman who is experiencing an irregular cycle can both make use of the phases of the Moon to regulate their own experience. The dark of the Moon is a time for intro-spection, moving into oneself and experiencing visions; the New Moon is a good time to begin new projects, to start to bring that inward vision out into the light. The Full Moon is the time to be creative and to allow your inspiration to be manifested and made known; it is also the time to interact with and be energetic in the world. The last quarter then brings things to fruition and begins again the cycle of introspection and extroversion, reception and activity.

MOOD/EMOTIONS

As mood fluctuations can sometimes be both violent and sudden, it may be necessary to make several separate notes under 'mood/emotions' during the day, and then to explore these more fully in the expanded journal. The journal is a strictly personal record and can be kept confidential, so be as honest as possible here and, when making the additional entries, write fully without pause or censoring.

If you really did feel like killing the milkman over the mix-up about the daily pinta, then say so – the single word 'murderous' will suffice, anything longer should be reserved for the expanded journal. If you had a panic attack at the supermarket checkout, make a note of it and then explore as fully as possible the reasons for the attack, writing down everything that comes up for you, no matter how trivial or unimportant it may seem, as somewhere there will be a clue to the underlying beliefs or difficulties which are being triggered (usually deepseated questions of value or self-worth). If you spent the morning in floods of tears for no apparent reason, exploring this in your journal may well reveal the hidden cause.

Very often, fully describing a seemingly unbearable emotion will help to dissipate it and reduce the amount of energy you invest in warding it off or keeping it 'under control' – which usually means out of awareness, a situation which inevitably stores up difficulties for the future. Equally, once you have explored the feelings, you may well find that they have a valid basis and that an appropriate change needs to be made to accommodate how you feel. Your journal entry may well then enable you to express your feelings to anyone else involved, and to define the kind of change, support, understanding, and so forth that you require. Similarly, if you felt incredibly randy or totally off sex, then record it. Knowing at what stage in your cycle you feel like making love can be helpful in avoiding sexual 'rejection' problems between you and and your partner. If you can clearly say: 'I'm really not feeling like it right now but I know that in a few days [or whenever] this will have passed', then communication with your partner is less likely to break down and you are more likely to receive what you need when you need it. Similarly, if you have a strong urge for sex, then a way can be found to meet it whether you have a partner or not (see Chapter 5).

And remember, don't only record the 'bad' feelings. Expressions of joy and normality will help to convince you that it is not all doom and gloom, even though it often feels like it. Deliberately seeking to make a previously stipulated number of 'good' entries each day helps you to identify what is going well, and aids in formulating a more positive approach to life – an approach which pays dividends in terms of a deeper sense of well-being. This type of positive entry is especially useful when underlying depression is an ongoing symptom as it helps to focus attention away from the drain of negative and pessimistic thoughts, resulting in greater resources of energy and a sense that there will be a future after all. The beautiful 'Bouquets for Ruth' idea at the end of the chapter can also be used to build confidence and self-esteem, and to chart your uniquely individual passage through the menopause.

This particular journal entry (or the one on dreams) may well also be the one which enables you to catch the fleeting stray thought which epitomizes the ancestral attitude you are unknowingly carrying (see Chapter 4). The deep depression of 'It's all downhill from here on' echoes generations of women whose 'useful life' ended with the cessation of their fertility, despite the often welcomed break from the endless round of childbearing and raising, and who frequently lacked either the energy or the resources to take proper care of themselves, thereby quickly sliding into old age and forgetfulness. You may well be unconsciously living out this or some other pattern and reflecting it in weight gain, tiredness and loss of purpose. Identifying the underlying belief through exploration of the presenting problem or thought empowers you to take steps to change the programming.

SITUATION

This entry enables you to make the link between what is taking place in your life and what is happening in your body. Notes such as 'work – boring', 'important meeting', '. . . away/came home', 'new date', 'big row' can be important clues in assessing how your menopausal symptoms are a response to your life situation.

The effect of stress is well documented and the release of adrenaline during stress can place an additional, sometimes intolerable, strain on a body which is already out of balance and trying to cope with hormonal fluctuations. Therefore, identifying times of stress, which are often the joyful occasions of life just as much as the difficult, can be helpful in foreseeing and mitigating problems. Allowing time for extra relaxation, or pampering yourself with a massage, can be vital in allaying the effects of stress, as can avoiding, whenever possible, situations which create it. Relaxing for as little as fifteen minutes a day can be extremely helpful in counteracting stress and a simple relaxation exercise is included in Appendix I.

SYMPTOMS

Anything which is not usual for you should be noted as a symptom. This includes the more obvious menopausal problems such as hot flushes and vaginal dryness, but should also include details like 'aching shoulders', 'constipation', 'flatulence', 'loss of memory', 'speech problems', 'gum disease', 'dry skin', 'spots', etc.

This entry should be closely monitored over a period of time and compared with the 'food' entry to see if there is a consistent pattern, as the occasional 'loss' of a word, for instance, can be a symptom of a food allergy as well as a hormonal problem. Similarly, by continuously checking the 'treatments' entry, it is possible to tell which symptoms are being successfully treated, and what has brought about the improvement.

SLEEP

Sleep disturbances and insomnia are common menopausal problems, and can be closely related to symptoms such as night sweats or depression and to hormonal levels or stress. There is usually an underlying pattern to be perceived, such as an increasing problem in remaining asleep in the week leading up to a period and then a gradual tailing back into normal sleep for the remainder of the cycle, for example.

If such patterns can be identified, then it is possible to use natural methods, such as hypnosis or herbs, to counter-act them. Any nights which do not fit the underlying pattern will be quickly identified and should be checked against 'food' and 'situation' to find the cause.

DREAMS

The menopause can be a time of vivid dreaming, with intense and sometimes terrifying imagery which jolts the dreamer into heart-pounding wakefulness for the remainder of the night. These dreams may well link into the days just before a period starts, or to the Full Moon if you live in a place where the Moon's light can affect you. Therefore, the menopause journal can help you to anticipate dreams and you could keep a notebook and pen by your bed to record them.

These dreams are the symbolic language of the sub-conscious mind and a dream diary may well reveal the underlying message which is being relayed from the depths of consciousness. Such a message may be concerned with fears or hopes for the future, or it could be a re-run of events or beliefs from the past which still have a hold on the present. Either way, writing out the dream in the pres-ent tense while it is still fresh in your mind and then adding all the fears, feelings, associations and expectations which the dream brings up can help to clarify the imagery. As the dreams can include characters from one's own immedi-ate family, often taking very upsetting roles, it can be helpful to see these figures as portraying a part of yourself of which you may not be aware, rather than necessarily relating to the actual person.

This substitution was particularly helpful in the dreams of a pre-menopausal woman who kept dreaming that her daughter had somehow 'lost' her husband and young daughter and was now wandering pointlessly through life, desperately seeking other outlets whilst denying what had happened. This dream directly related to the woman's own younger self and the loss of her hopes for the future, and the cessation of biological fertility which was approaching, coupled with a loss of purpose with regard to her own non-biological creativity.

Dreams may also include helpful messages from the subconscious, albeit often in terms which also need decoding. These may vary from hints about foods, supplements or exercise to more specific items. Some dreams are more explicit: a woman dreamed that she and her mother were walking along a rough road over mountains carrying huge burdens. When she looked back, the road was smooth and flat and she realized that all their difficulties were of their own making – and also that she was carrying the burden of her mother's beliefs which were making her own pathway more difficult than necessary.

FOOD

The food we eat can be directly related to the moods and 'diseases' we experience and many menopausal symptoms are linked to, or aggravated by, what we take into our bodies. Chocolate, for example, is a natural antidepressant (which is why it is so often craved during pre-menstrual tension or depression) but it also contains caffeine, which can greatly increase mastitis (inflammation of the breasts) and insomnia. Coffee, quite apart from its effect on sleep, also plays a part in hot flushes and anxiety states. By logging the number of cups of tea, coffee, alcohol, etc. and the type of foods eaten, it is possible to pick up the links between food allergy or aggravation and the symptoms produced and to vary the diet accordingly.

People are often surprised at just how many drinks they unwittingly consume in a day, and how unbalanced their diet can be. Sugar, particularly the 'hidden' sugar content in food, may well be aggravating an underlying blood sugar imbalance, the signs of which can closely resemble some of the menopausal symptoms. By adjusting the diet to include a greater quantity of slow-release carbohydrates, such as rice or wholegrain bread or pasta, much of the lethargy associated with a sugar imbalance can be avoided. Similarly if a food allergy, such as the common wheat or dairy reaction, is identified, then the diet can be adjusted accordingly.

Many of the foods which would normally not cause difficulties, such as highly spiced foods, may need to be avoided during the menopause and others, which contain the calcium and vitamins so necessary at this time, may need to be increased. If herb teas such as sage (which stimulates hormones), peppermint (an aid to the digestive system) or bergamot (found in Earl Grey tea and useful for ameliorating hot flushes) are taken, these should be included under the 'treatments' section so that their effects can be monitored.

A useful detoxification diet is included in Appendix I. If food allergies are the basic problem, it will alleviate the symptoms and it has the added bonus of helping you to lose weight rapidly and without any of the usual cravings or hunger pangs. Foods should be gradually reintroduced and stopped immediately if any symptoms reappear. A food allergy will usually disappear if the food is completely avoided for a period of six months.

TREATMENTS

Treatments for menopausal symptoms are included in Chapters 1 and 2. However, unless a detailed record is kept, it is impossible to tell which are successful. This entry should also include any medication as it quickly identifies both positive changes and any unwanted effects which may arise and is particularly useful for anyone taking HRT, tranquillizers, antidepressants or sleeping tablets. Exercise or treatments such as acupuncture or massage should also be entered so that the effect on sleep, mood and physical symptoms can be monitored.

It is important to bear in mind that natural treatments may take some time to begin working, so the effects may be noticed over a period of weeks rather than days. Equally a 'healing challenge' may also arise which will require recording.

WORKING WITH THE JOURNAL INFORMATION

It is essential to review all the entries regularly each month in order to obtain maximum benefit from the information recorded. In this way it is possible to gain an objective assessment of your own personal situation. Once your individual patterns are identified, you can choose a time to partake vigorously of life, or an appropriate period in which to withdraw into yourself and your inner life, emerging refreshed at a new stage in the cycle. The appropriate action can be taken either to remove the cause of or to counteract the symptoms experienced and to deal with any underlying beliefs which you expose.

You may find it helpful to avoid particular foods and to take specific herbal treatments or supplements in the week leading up to a period or to adjust your activities to fit in with times of maximum energy, for instance. You can also monitor your progress in handling stress, learning relaxation, and developing an exercise programme suited to your needs, and note the effect on your symptoms. You can learn to attune to the rhythm of your own sexuality, following its peaks and troughs and entering into a more fulfilling and satisfactory sexual phase.

Once you have been keeping a journal for at least six months, long enough to establish the patterns, you may prefer to note only items of special interest in the day-to-day journal, such as the trial reintroduction of a food, for example, or a new supplement or herbal treatment, or a particularly vivid phase of dreaming. However, as the effects of the expanded journal are so therapeutic, it can be useful to continue this as and when the need arises, particularly as it charts your progress through the transition into the Wise Woman.

If you belong to a self-help group, the journal can provide a basis for discussion and sharing of experiences, and the practice gained in writing up your feelings will facilitate sharing these within a group. It can also be extremely useful to telephone contacts from the group at recognized stress points in the month, as this provides both support and an outlet for 'irrational' feelings you may be experiencing at this time. If there is no self-help group in your area, you might like to consider starting one.

If you are having any form of counselling, then the journal information can be invaluable in pinpointing your particular cycle of response and in identifying the feelings which are arising from the past and the messages your subconscious mind may be sending you via dreams. It also makes it possible to recognize where moods are symptomatic of changes required in your life situation.

'BOUQUETS FOR RUTH'

This beautiful idea came from a lovely, and loving, lady who has completed her transition into a truly Wise Woman. When she was twenty Ruth entered a totally enclosed order of nuns 'to become good enough'. After seventeen years of growing spiritually she was filled with so much love that she had to share it with people. Sadly, this was not encouraged within her order and she had to return to the outside world.

When she left the order, however, she found that she had totally lost herself as a person. She was afraid to look in a mirror, cried whenever anyone looked at her, and her self-esteem was at an all-time low. She had to rediscover her body and her femininity, which had been severely repressed during the convent years, and find out 'who Ruth really was'.

During the process of finding herself she invented 'Bouquets for Ruth'. Every time anyone gave her anything, she took a picture of it and mounted the photo in a special book. Whenever anyone said anything nice about her, she wrote it down in the book with the name and the date beside it. Then, when she doubted herself or was depressed, she would turn to her 'Bouquets' and tell herself that she 'really wasn't that bad, after all: so and so had said this or given her that'.

This idea can easily be incorporated into the menopause journal and could also include photographs taken at significant stages in the journey so that you can see the transition taking place and chart the changes from your face and body posture. It is a wonderfully supportive and nurturing gift for yourself, one which you will treasure and return to again and again in the years to come.

4. ❋ Overcoming the Past

If a large section of the population is viewed as unstable, irrational, crippled, depressed or as a figure of fun, they can be dismissed as inferior and need not be taken seriously.[1]

Myra Hunter

INHERITED BELIEFS

When I was fourteen and my mother thirty-six, I was surprised to find a magazine article about the menopause lying on my bed. So began a 'menopause' that lasted for seventeen years. I absorbed, without knowing it, an attitude of martyrdom; this was the inevitable price one paid for being a woman. Looking back, I think I suspected even then that what was happening was not so much a menopause as a prolonged life crisis which my mother resolutely refused to face.

I was determined that, for me, things would be different. Having started to menstruate at the age of 9½, with all the attendant social and peer difficulties that brought, and having had a traumatic pregnancy which gave me a daughter but made it inadvisable that I should even contemplate having more children, for me the menopause spelt freedom. No more contraception, no more tampons to dispose of in unsuitable foreign plumbing. What a release!

The discovery of the book *The Wise Wound*[2] came rather too late in my life to change my view of menstruation, although the book was a light shining into a place that had been dark for too long. Intellectually I could understand the need to reunite with the blood roots of my femaleness and rediscover the hidden energies of my Moon cycle but I failed to make the connection at a feeling level. To me menstruation was a nuisance, and the sooner it was over the better, particularly as I viewed the time following menopause as the time I would become more, rather than less, creative.

Imagine my surprise, therefore, when, faced with the sudden onset of symptoms that appeared to have only one meaning, I found myself repeating all the old negative conditioning. 'What do you expect at your age?', I caught myself thinking. Doomful nightmares left me unable to sleep and a vicious cycle of insomnia found me wrung out and listless for days on end. I became immobile through a 'hormone induced' backache and physical symptoms too numerous to mention. And those deep black depressions when the end of the world seemed nigh. What horror; I was falling apart!

On a day when I was seeing more clearly than most, I sat down and listed everything I could remember from my childhood that pertained to the menopause and compared it with what I thought, as an enlightened woman of today, I believed. I realized just how deeply that 1950s article with its gloomy predictions of unavoidable physical and mental decline had etched into my consciousness, and recognized how I was repeating my mother's pattern of unlived life manifesting as 'symptoms' of 'The Change'.

I recognized how superficial are the things we think we have learned, as opposed to those things we do not realize we have learned, and how strongly entrenched repetitive patterns can be. Fortunately, I also brought back to mind the concept of 'reframing' beliefs and this greatly aided my transition into a more positive attitude.

Since that time, talking to many women undergoing the same experience, I have realized that, as women, we need to free ourselves not only from the stereotyped roles to which our culture condemns us, but also from the cycle of ancestral beliefs which we inherit and unconsciously live out literally 'at gut level' through the menstrual cycle – particularly as it moves towards its close.

The following exercises will help you to identify the messages from your past which are still having a deep, although usually unrecognized effect on your present life. Do take the time to write down your answers and do not censor anything that comes to mind. It is usually the very thing that makes us think 'Oh no, I can't possibly believe this' that is the key we are seeking to unlock the past.

THE LIFE STATEMENT

When assessing how the past is interacting with the present, it can be extremely useful to make a brief statement of where you are in your life and what is happening around you now. This is not so much a statement of *how* you are, although this can be included, as *who* you are and what your present experience of being a woman is.

As well as specific information about your role(s) in life and how these differ from the essential you, you might want to include, for example, whether you are in a relationship and how permanent this is. If you have children, you could say what is happening with them and how this affects your life. You could also add details of the extended family; whether your mother and grandmother are still alive, for instance, and what your relationship with them is like.

EXERCISE

Make a life statement

THE FAMILY MYTH

Most families have a myth about menstruation that is handed down through the female line. In the families of many women now reaching their forties and fifties, menstruation was something secret and somehow unclean that had to be hidden from the world. For untold numbers of women it was a curse or a necessary evil (a view that was usually also applied to sex). For others it had only one function: reproduction. A friend related her sex education experience from her school days: a mistress described menstruation as 'the bloody tears of a disappointed womb'. No doubt here about the pain, anguish and disappointment symbolized by the monthly bleeding for this unfortunate lady.

If your mother and her mother before her believed that it was a time of pain, then this is most likely what it became for you. Similarly, if you never had time, or space, for dreams, for reflections, for going inward, then you probably suffered from debilitating PMS and heavy bleeding. For the victims of 'the curse', the menopause can be a time of release, although, never having learned to enjoy being truly female, the release may be into something androgynous or male-emulating rather than into a liberating feminine energy. Interest in sex may also be 'expected' to decline or diminish and life, far from beginning at forty, ends at fifty leaving little to look forward to. Unfortunately, for many women whose myth is that of 'necessary evil', the menopause can unconsciously signal the end of their function as a woman.

For women whose myth was that menstruation and self-esteem are linked to sexuality and desirability, the menopausal experience may perpetuate the experience of 'being in heat' as a way of proving desirability (leading to extended hot flushes, for instance), or a desperate seeking after youth (often actively competing with their daughters to prove how desirable they still are).

For a few, much more fortunate women, menstruation was something to enjoy, a symbol of womanhood that linked them to their essential femaleness. However, the very specialness of menstruation for these women can create difficulties during the menopause as they may feel that, in losing this symbol of woman-ness, they are losing their identity as a woman.

EXERCISE

1. Spend a few moments identifying your family myth about menstruation.
2. Consider how this could affect your menopause.

HOW YOU VIEW THE MENOPAUSE

To begin untangling your beliefs, it is helpful to make a list of what you think you believe about the menopause.

This should include all your positive and negative feelings, attitudes, beliefs, fears and hopes. Take plenty of time and include everything that comes into your mind, no matter how much it may conflict with what you think you ought to feel and believe. (Divide the page in half lengthways and leave the right-hand column blank.)

EXERCISE

Describe how you view the menopause.

IDENTIFYING INHERITED BELIEFS

Write down everything you have ever heard your mother, or other family members, say about 'The Change' or 'It's her age, you know'. Include anything you may have read during your formative years. Allow yourself at least fifteen to twenty minutes for this information to rise into consciousness and keep writing even when you think you have found everything. The beliefs with the strongest hold are often the most deeply buried and unconscious.

Include everything, no matter how ridiculous or obvious. One woman found that she believed that menopausal women were inevitably driven to madness and 'unspeakable acts' because an aunt of hers had had an affair which resulted in a nervous breakdown during the menopause. Spoken of in hushed whispers whenever the adults thought the children weren't listening, this had profoundly affected her view of menopausal women.

Be sure to list the positive beliefs as well as the negative ones. (Divide the page in half lengthways and leave the right-hand column blank.)

EXERCISE

Identify your inherited beliefs.

REFRAMING INHERITED BELIEFS

Now read through your list of inherited beliefs. By identifying the incongruities and conflicts of 'inherited beliefs', it is possible to begin to separate what works for you from what is no longer relevant, and you may find several inherited beliefs that you emphatically disagree with and need to put a cross by immediately. On the other hand, there may be some beliefs that you want to keep. In this case, simply tick the right-hand column.

For many of these beliefs, however, there will be a 'pay-off' involved even if it is only in conforming and not running counter to the family system. A pay-off is a hidden, and usually unacknowledged, benefit which accrues from holding that belief. For example, if you have always disliked sex, then seeing the menopause as a time when sexual attractiveness and libido markedly decline tends to produce the pay-off of less sexual activity. Similarly, the symptoms of night sweats can be used as an excuse for moving into separate beds. Many people will share the pay-off of becoming a 'has-been', which is to be totally free to do and be as little as possible – much less demanding than changing, particularly as change can be a deeply paralysing experience for many people.

Some pay-offs can involve power struggles, particularly in relationship issues, and you may have to forego a feeling of being in control, particularly where your physical symptoms are, seemingly, making something happen (or not, as the case may be). Sex, for instance, frequently becomes an unconscious weapon in the battle between the sexes and, if you need to feel you are in control, then you may find that your body apparently dictates the pattern of sexual interaction.

EXERCISE

Identify the pay-offs for as many of your inherited beliefs as possible in the blank right-hand column and decide whether you are prepared to forego the pay-off for each of them, marking with a cross where appropriate. If you decide you cannot forego the pay-off, then obviously this belief is still working for you and the belief should be ticked.

Then take all the items on the list that have a cross beside them and consider how you can change the way you see this belief. You may need to make a positive affirmation out of a previously negative statement, such as changing 'A woman is no longer sexually desirable after the menopause' to 'Now that I am free from the burden of contraception, I am free to explore my sexuality in new and exciting ways'. The woman who linked madness to the menopause discovered that she could attune to 'creative madness' in which her old 'rules' structure was dissolved and she was freed to become much more innovative and creative, indulging in acts which her family thought were 'unspeakable' whilst she remained unconcerned about their censure.

Or you may find that you need to identify a real benefit, rather than a pay-off, from a statement. For instance, moving into your own room, rather than sharing a bed, could become an opportunity to have more time for yourself and to choose when to share intimate moments with your partner, thus improving the quality of the time you spend together.

1. Work on your list.
2. Create a new family myth, setting out how you now wish to view menstruation and the menopause.
3. If appropriate, share this with your daughter.

REFRAMING YOUR ATTITUDE TO THE MENOPAUSE

The reframing exercise above should be carried out for all the non-constructive or negative statements on your 'how you view the menopause' list, transforming them into positive statements. For instance, if you have always seen the menopause as 'the end', the positive affirmation would be 'All possibilities are open to me'.

You may well find that you identify statements which are based on a need for changes to be made in your life. If you are not happy with your sexual pattern, for instance, or if you feel you need more help in the house or would like to change, or take up, a career, etc., then the next section can be helpful and you may like to move on to that before completing the reframing below.

EXERCISE

Reframe your beliefs.

MAKING CHANGES

If you identify something in your life that needs to change, it can be helpful to plan how you will achieve this change.

EXERCISE

Without stopping to work out if they are practical, write down as many ways of achieving your goal as possible. This 'brainstorming' approach may well throw up an unexpected solution as it involves the unconscious and intuitive parts of your mind as well as the rational thought process. It is particularly appropriate if you wish to make a major life style change but have no idea where to begin.

1.   List all the changes you want to make.
2.   Select one or two to work on first.
3.   Set a date to begin.

CHANGE AND THE 'THREE-PART ASSERTION MESSAGE'

If your change involves another person, the way you communicate this need for change will affect how well it is received. The 'three-part assertion message' can be useful here as it clearly states a position without laying blame. Part 1 sets out the 'when' or the 'what' of the situation; For example, 'When I stay at home all day . . .'. Part 2 sets out what happens: '. . . I get bored . . .', and Part 3 how you feel about it: '. . . and I feel miserable and unfulfilled'. You can then go on to state the change you would like: 'I would therefore like to train for a career which will utilize my talents and I would appreciate your support while I do this'.

The advantage of this method is that it focuses on making the change, and does not become sidetracked by arguing or laying blame for the situation that has arisen. It offers the other person a clear message, which they can accept or reject. The difficulty is that they may reject what you are saying, in which case you have to decide whether to go ahead anyway! If the need for change has been contributing to your menopausal 'symptoms', then it is important that (unless you are going ahead unilaterally) you find a way to a mutually acceptable compromise or an alternative means of having your need met. This will necessitate further consideration and negotiation but the same three-part message should be used to avoid entering into an argument.

EXERCISE

1. State the change you would like to make.
2. List the steps you can take to achieve this.
3. Set a date for commencing.
4. Set out how you will communicate this change.

USING AFFIRMATIONS

An affirmation is a positive statement phrased in the 'now', not in future. The secret for successful affirming is to ensure that the affirmation does not include a negative phrase, and to 'act as if'. So that, instead of saying 'I am going to become. . . .' or 'I am no longer . . .', the present tense is used: 'I am . . .'. If one of your statements about the menopause was, for instance, 'I am no longer attractive', this could become a positive affirmation: 'I am an attractive woman who has a fulfilling and exciting relationship'. This 'reprogrammes' the subconscious part of the mind, which will then make the necessary changes. We all tend to attract to ourselves what we expect so, by reprogramming any pessimistic, negative thoughts, we will attract more positive life-enhancing experiences through our affirmations.

Affirmations can be written, spoken, read or heard, according to which sense you feel most comfortable with. Some women are touch-orientated and writing is particularly appropriate for them as the movements kinesthetically programme the mind. Others prefer to use their eyes or ears repetitiously.

Select one or two affirmations and set aside a definite

time each day and write, read or speak the affirmation(s) as many times as possible for no longer than a five minute period (do not allot too much time as you may become bored, which is counter-productive). The more you use the affirmations, the sooner the reprogramming will take place and you will soon recognize how many times a day would be appropriate, and convenient, for you.

It can also be helpful to write out the affirmation and fix it in some place where you can gaze at it from time to time. Speaking the affirmations aloud is preferable to reading them to yourself, so you may need to select your time and place carefully but if you do read them, then do so slowly and rhythmically.

One of the most useful ways of practising affirmations, particularly if you travel on public transport, is to record them onto a tape which you then play to yourself. The tape could incorporate music in the background as this can aid assimilation. This tape method is also highly effective when used last thing at night and can be combined with the instruction to fall into a deep and peaceful sleep.

You will probably need to practise the affirmations regularly for at least a fortnight before you notice any appreciable difference but, given time, they do work and can dramatically change your life. Once you have worked with your first set and can see the difference, select one or two more affirmations and begin to use these. Repeat this until you have worked through your list.

EXERCISE

1.   Write out your list of affirmations.
2.   Select one or two to begin working with.
3.   Practise your affirmations regularly.

THE FAIRY GODMOTHER

We all have within us hopes and aspirations, dreams of what we could be. And we all have within us the means of bringing these into being. This exercise identifies our deepest hopes, and offers an opportunity of manifesting these.

EXERCISE

1. Given an absolutely free choice, list what you wish for yourself and what you would like to do.
2. What is stopping you?

Are you making negative assumptions that are holding you back? For example, do you think that: 'I'm not intelligent enough', 'There'll never be enough money', 'I've got responsibilities', 'You can't do that at my age', etc.?

3. If so, can you reframe these into positive statements?
4. What steps could you take to achieve your dream?
5. Are you able to commit yourself to making at least one of your dreams come true?

Now, close your eyes and relax for a moment. Imagine that you have just met your Fairy Godmother and she has agreed to grant your wish or make your dream come true. How do you feel? Are you apprehensive or excited, joyful, eager to start, full of anticipation? Do you have passion and enthusiasm for the project? Can you commit yourself fully to bringing about this dream?

If your answer is no, do you have hidden reservations or fears? If so, you may need to do some more reframing and affirmations to clear away the negative attitudes.

If your answer is yes, then put the passion and enthusiasm to work; start planning right away how you can achieve your dearest wish.

6. Set out your plans.
7. Set a commencing date.

DEALING WITH FEAR

It is a truism that none of us knows what we are capable of until we try, and yet so many of us allow fear to hold us back. Most of the fear is past conditioning and you will have dealt with much of that by working through this chapter. If we can feel the fear, put it to one side, and start anyway, who knows what we will achieve.

It is now many years since I was told that I would lecture in public. The prospect terrified me! The time came, however, when I agreed to do so. Fortunately a friend told me how he had overcome fear. The secret lay in not denying the fear but acknowledging it was there, seeing it as a little grey furry animal in need of love and reassurance.

I made this image real. My daughter had a little furry stuffed toy which had become grey and amorphous through the years. I put this grey animal in my bag and, when I entered the lecture hall, placed it under the lectern and petted it from time to time. My knees were knocking, I held myself up on the lectern, but I managed to talk coherently to 250 people and no other lecture or workshop has ever held quite the same terror as that one!

MOURNING THE PAST

What a blessing to take time to integrate loss into our lives.[3]

Edith Mize

Having worked through the exercises in the first part of this chapter, you will have come a long way towards changing how you view the past but you may still be carrying the burden of history. We all have things in the past which we regret or grieve for. We may resent not having had the chance to go to university; we regret not taking that challenging job; marrying or not marrying. We grieve for the child that never was, the opportunity we missed, the part of our body that has been taken away. We are angry at old abuse, at our mother for teaching us that a woman's place was in the home and that men's needs should be put above our own. We may yearn for perfect love, crave fame or wealth.

Whatever our own particular package of regrets, the menopause provides the ideal time for honouring these and laying them to rest so that they no longer interfere in the working of the present. The mourning process is a process of release, and it has many stages including sadness, denial, guilt, anger and resolution. True grieving allows all the emotions to be clearly felt and, surprisingly perhaps, because the feelings are validated rather than suppressed, mourning need not occupy a long period of time to be effective. It is the quality of the experience, rather than the quantity, which is healing.

Unfortunately, in most western cultures, grief and mourning have been seen as something to 'get over' (or avoid) rather than as a valid and necessary part of human life. However, we all die many small deaths throughout our life and if we do not acknowledge, and grieve for, the changes signified by our smaller deaths, then we will carry with us the burden of unresolved grief.

The Rite of Mourning offers the opportunity of working through that grief and mourning the past. It requires uninterrupted time in which you can allow yourself to feel and express all the emotions attached to the old grief. You should give yourself all the time and support you need, so you may have to negotiate with a partner or find someone to care for your children in order to have space for yourself.

If you have a history of abuse (emotional or physical), addiction or depression, then it would be sensible to talk over what you are intending to do with a counsellor and ask them to work through the exercises with you or to be available by phone in the event that memories arise which are too difficult for you to handle. Similarly, if you are involved in a self-help group, it would be useful to know that one person will be available for you to phone should you need support, or you could work through this chapter together in the group. (It would seem wise for anyone undertaking mourning work to have someone to contact just in case something major does surface unexpectedly. If you do not have anyone else available, the Samaritans will always provide a listening ear.) It can also be helpful to talk over what arises during this exercise with an understanding friend or counsellor.

Ideally, you should set aside a weekend of solitude and it may be helpful to return physically to the scene of your greatest regrets; booking into a small hotel in a place you used to live, for example, to reconnect to the experiences you had there. If it is not possible to be physically present, don't worry, a mental recap of your life will trigger memories and connections.

You should prepare for the mourning rite carefully, gathering together old photographs, letters or diaries, tissues, plenty of paper, your favourite food, a much-loved teddy, some flowers, a candle, and such like. Leave the phone off the hook and ensure that you are in a warm, comfortable room. Whilst being cold and hungry or lonely may re-create your old feelings, it will not facilitate letting go of the past and although one or two drinks may help you to open up, more should be avoided as alcohol can dull the pain and suppress what you are trying to honour, as do nicotine or drugs.

The homoeopathic remedy Ignatia can greatly aid the mourning process. It is recommended that the 200x potency be taken half-hourly for three doses before beginning this work. If the grief is very old or well buried, and particularly if this is causing symptoms such as depression, a 6x potency could also be taken three times a day for the week before the rite.

RETURNING TO THE PAST

If you have physically returned to a place you knew, spend a few hours wandering the streets and gazing at your old home. If there is someone else who was intimately involved and who could help you remember at this time, then arrange to talk to them and explain why you are doing this and what you need to know. When you have absorbed the atmosphere and reconnected to that old you, return to your base so that you can allow the feelings to flow freely.

Old photographs, letters and diaries are extremely useful aids in returning to the past and may well remind you of things you, but not your subconscious mind, have forgot-ten. You may like to gather together mementoes of the past to create a 'Personal History' scrapbook which honours who you were. Old memories, and particularly old pain, can cause a tightening in the solar plexus area, with a consequent holding-in of the breath so remember to breathe easily during this review, allowing any emotions or mem-ories to rise gently to the surface so that you can view them objectively. The idea here is not to punish yourself, just to acknowledge what has been.

Spend some time in reverie, idly reviewing the past but not consciously seeking any part of it. Try to scan the whole of your experience, the pleasure and the pain, from birth, or beyond, to the present moment. You may feel an urgent need to record, and reframe, certain scenes, or to explore the emotion by writing in your journal. Or you may prefer to make notes for future work. Give yourself as much time as you need to reconnect to the past but don't allow yourself so long that you begin to wallow in self-pity – an attack of the 'poor me's' or 'if onlies' is not conducive to emotional release.

REGRETS FROM THE PAST

When you have had sufficient time, fill in all your regrets as quickly as possible and without any prior thought, leaving the right-hand column blank. Don't censor; include anything, no matter how trivial or damning it may appear (remembering that you are the only person who will ever read it unless you choose otherwise). Your list might include things like 'not being a boy', 'being born at all', 'not saying no', 'marrying because I had to', 'not studying harder', 'not getting that job', 'not having a child', 'having too many children', 'losing myself', 'getting divorced', 'losing touch with old friends', 'that abortion', 'that row with my mother', 'those cruel things I said', 'allowing myself (or others) to be abused', 'being abusive', etc.

If you have had surgery, particularly for the removal of a breast or the womb, there may well be a great deal of anger and grief locked up from that time. The loss of a part of the body, especially those parts intimately connected with being female, may, unless adequate counselling and support was available at the time, leave an 'emotional hole' that is still in need of healing. If this is the case, be sure to work through the exercises on loss and anger as well as including all your regrets here.

EXERCISE

List your regrets from the past.

REGRETS ABOUT THE MENOPAUSE

Then, without pausing, list everything you have regretted about the menopause, again leaving the right-hand column blank. You may find that you include statements like, 'My usefulness is over', 'No one will want me anymore', 'My creative life is over', 'I'm now middle aged', 'I will miss my menstrual cycle', 'I'm not a woman any longer', etc.

You may well find that some items appear on both lists. If, for example, you always wanted another child, then it is most likely that loss of fertility will be a major regret connected with the menopause and if you regret not training for a career, it is possible that you may regard the menopause as 'too late' rather than as a time of new opportunity. For many women, regrets from the past are to do with relationships (either those that were entered into or those that were not) and this too may be linked to seeing the menopause as a time of diminishing physical and sexual attractiveness.

EXERCISE

List your regrets about the menopause.

WORKING WITH THE LISTS

Now spend some time reading through the lists in an accepting, non-judgemental way, acknowledging that this is how you feel, or felt at the time. Then, take each item in turn and decide whether this is something you need to mourn, something that could be reframed into a benefit or a goal for the future, or something that needs forgiveness or reparation, etc. and note this in the right-hand column. If a particular emotion, such as anger or sadness, is attached to the regret, this should also be noted.

Some statements may need to be included in several categories. For example, 'My creative life has ended' is a statement that your loss of biological creativity may need to be mourned. It can, however, be reframed as 'My biological creativity has ended and I am free to explore my creativity in other ways', or made into a goal: 'I allow my previously unfulfilled writing/art/music/design/etc. talents to come to the fore by taking classes (etc.), starting on. . . .' It is important to stipulate a time for beginning to work on your goal and to ensure that you adhere to this. You may also like to set a time limit for the goal to be achieved.

Begin by making a separate list of all the things you have identified as needing to mourn. Then gather together anything you feel angry about and place them on a separate list. Make a further list of anything you are sad about, then move on to anything you feel a need to make reparation for or the things for which forgiveness is required. Finally, make a list of all the things you need to reframe or to turn into goals.

If time is limited, move on to the mourning ritual outlined later in the chapter and work through the remainder of the exercises applicable to you at a more convenient time. If time is not limited, take one list of regrets at a time and work through the exercises below that are appropriate. (NOTE: It is only necessary to work through the exercises for items that appear on your lists.)

THE BACH FLOWER REMEDIES

The Bach Flower Remedies, which are available from many health food shops, can considerably aid in the release of old emotions. The remedies, which allow a gentle, non-invasive dissolution of old feelings to take place, should be taken at least three times a day for several weeks to ensure a total clearance. I have found that the most lasting effect is obtained by using the remedy undiluted. However, as the remedies include brandy, anyone with a drink problem should always dilute the remedies so that only one or two drops are put into a small bottle of pure water, and two or three drops taken from this.

WORKING WITH ANGER

Unresolved anger often lies at the heart of depression, addiction and lethargy as it saps vital energy by the very strength needed to keep it suppressed. It is usually experienced as an underlying mental or physical pain which surfaces whenever that control is relaxed. During the mood fluctuations of the menopause, this old pain has an opportunity to reach awareness and the menopause itself often engenders anger along with a sense of loss.

If you are suffering from unresolved anger which has festered into resentment then it is extremely likely that you will be suffering from physical symptoms as well. Freeing yourself from this old anger can dramatically improve your well-being. The Bach Remedy Willow will release resentment whilst Holly is appropriate for angry feelings based on jealousy, hatred or envy.

When working with anger there are two simple decisions which will allow you to release from it: to either accept what has happened, or do something to change the situation. Anger can also be 'withheld knowledge' and it can be the key to discovering the changes you need to make in your life. Doing something about anger may involve confronting another person and, during your mourning period, this should be in the form of a letter which clearly states what happened, how you felt about it and what the result was. For example, a letter to an ex-husband who ran off with your best friend might need to say that you felt angry and betrayed, used, no longer attractive, sad at the loss of friendship, and so forth, and that this adversely affected your image of yourself to the extent that either you were unable to make new relationships, or that you then became compulsive in your attempt to convince yourself that you were still attractive – or whatever was true for you. A letter to the surgeon who carried out an operation can convey the anger, helplessness and frustration you experienced; how invaded and alien your body felt; the loss of your femininity, and the lack of understanding, disgust and rejection you believed you were receiving from others. Even if you do not intend to post the letter, you will still gain considerable release from writing it.

EXERCISE

Take each item from your 'anger' list in turn and complete the following:

1. Write the statement: 'I am angry about. . . .'
2. Are you prepared to do something about it?

If 'yes', move on to 3. If 'no', are you able to let go of the situation and release yourself from the effects, forgiving yourself if necessary for undergoing the experience? (Although it is vital to forgive yourself for your own part, it is desirable, but not necessary for your future well-being, to forgive the other person.) Forgiveness does not mean condoning or accepting the behaviour which made your angry. It does, however, involve letting go of what happened.

If you are able to let go at this stage, add it to the list of things to mourn and move on to another thing you are angry about. If you cannot, then you may need to put this particular issue aside until you can work through it with a trained counsellor or discuss it in your self-help group.

3. If 'yes', list everything you can do about it.
4. State the outcome you desire.
5. List the steps you will take.
6. Set a commencement date.

DISSOLVING RESENTMENT

Sometimes you may become aware of an underlying resentment which you cannot pin onto anything specific. It may be noticed through your thoughts or it may be more physically based. For instance, resentment may manifest as a vague feeling of 'something eating away at you' or a sense of 'clenching your abdomen' or 'holding onto something in your womb' which may relate to long-term sexual frustration or disappointment. The Bach Remedy Willow is appropriate for this condition and a simple visualization exercise can help to release this resentment. Visualizations use images which are created in the mind's eye and which speak to the subconscious levels of the mind. They should be carried out when relaxed, yet alert, preferably in a sitting position so that you do not fall asleep. The exercise should be taped, leaving plenty of time for following instructions, or, if you are working in a group, it could be read aloud by one of the members.

Sit in a comfortable position with your eyes closed and breathe gently and easily, withdrawing your awareness into yourself. Focus your mind on the spot just above and between your eyebrows. When you are relaxed and ready to begin, imagine yourself surrounded by a bubble of purple light, as though you are standing inside an amethyst crystal. [pause]

This bubble is magnetically charged and can draw the resentment into itself, so picture, and try to feel, the resentment leaving you and moving into the bubble. Make sure that you pay as much attention to drawing the resentment from behind you as you do to what is in front of you. [pause]

When all the resentment has been withdrawn, step out of the bubble and notice how light you feel without the burden of resentment. Allow the bubble to rise up high into the air until the warmth of the sun causes it to expand and burst, transforming your resentment into harmless droplets of light. [pause]

Then allow the warmth of the sun to purify and heal all the places where that resentment had lingered. [pause]

When you are ready, open your eyes and return your awareness to the room, taking time to adjust before moving.

WORKING WITH LOSS OR SADNESS

Unresolved sadness can provoke depression and many physical symptoms, and a sense of loss is often present at the menopause as many women feel that they are losing their femininity at this time. The Bach Remedy Star of Bethlehem is appropriate for sadness, but the combined 'Rescue Remedy' can also be used if deep shock has been part of the loss. The homoeopathic remedy Ignatia will also bring old feelings of loss to the surface so that they can be released.

Releasing these feelings makes way for new possibilities to emerge, particularly when unexpected benefits have been uncovered. You will probably never have connected the idea of benefit with loss before but identifying the benefit can be a key to unlocking the potential good in the situation, and with a little practice you can learn to see the benefit in any loss, no matter how great. This ability to find the benefit is closely linked to creativity. One of my clients expressed it as feeling very creative because she was always able to turn the most dire circumstances into blessings.

This exercise can be quite difficult if you have lost a loved one but it is helpful to dwell on the happy memories that remain and what your life with, or without, that person taught you. You may have needed a period of isolation to discover your own inner strength and independence, particularly if your old behaviour pattern was one of dependence. If the loss relates to a miscarriage or stillbirth, it can be even more difficult to see the benefit but it is usually possible at the very least to identify that you have experienced sadness and survived, gaining understanding and compassion for others who are in the same situation, for instance, and you may decide that you wish to share that empathy with others who are undergoing the same ordeal. If the loss relates to a part of your body, especially from cancer, then you may feel that you are able to offer hope and support to other women who are faced with the same prospect.

Taking each item in turn, write down in the fullest possible detail exactly what you feel you have lost and what the result of that loss was. Then consider what benefits may accrue to you following the loss and how you could put those benefits to use. Be sure to include any loss related to the menopause.

EXERCISE

1. Describe your loss or sadness as fully as possible.
2. How did that loss change you, or how do you feel it will change you?
3. Identify the benefits and what you learnt.
4. How can you use those benefits?
5. Set a date for commencing.

MAKING REPARATION

Guilt is a debilitating emotion (for which the appropriate Bach Remedy is Pine) and you may find something for which you would like to make reparation or ask forgiveness. It may simply be enough to apologize to the person concerned, to send some flowers perhaps, or drop them a line, or you may like to perform an appropriate service for that person as reparation. You will often find that the person concerned has forgotten all about the incident which has caused you so much remorse, so that forgiveness has been yours all along.

However, direct reparation is not always possible as it is so easy to lose track of people, or they may have died in the meantime. If this is the case, it is nevertheless very freeing to write the apology and you can use a photograph or the mind pictures of visualization to link to that person and express your regrets.

Women with a Catholic background may well find great relief in attending confession and receiving forgiveness but it is not necessary to be religious in order to find the spiritual peace which comes with forgiveness, as the forgiveness meditation below will show.

Finally, you may feel that you would like to perform an act of community service, for instance, or make some other gesture such as lighting a candle to symbolize clearing away the old guilt forever.

EXERCISE

1. Describe the act for which you wish to make reparation.
2. Are you able to make direct reparation?
3. Are you able to forgive yourself for this action? (If 'no', make a note to discuss with a friend or your self-help group).
4. Are you prepared to receive forgiveness?
5. Write a letter explaining exactly how you feel now and what you seek from the other person (forgiveness, etc.). If possible, copy this letter out and mail it as soon as possible.
6. List anything you would like to do by way of reparation.
7. Date(s) by which you will do the above.

FORGIVENESS

Guided visualizations can be extremely helpful in releasing emotions and 'reprogramming' your response to situations.

The following visualizations should be recorded onto a tape with appropriate pauses for carrying out the instructions, or read through until you can remember them clearly. If a group is undertaking the visualization, one person should be selected to read them slowly, giving everyone time to form the images in their mind and allowing plenty of time to carry out the instructions.

Some people may find difficulty in visualizing (seeing the images) and, as music can help images to form, suitable music could be played softly in the background but should not be allowed to become intrusive. However, if you do not 'see' an image then you can 'act as if'; it is the intention that counts in these meditations so you can feel yourself 'seeing' even though actual images might not arise.

You may like to complete the meditation by burning the letter from the exercise above in a ceremonial way, lighting a candle or placing a flower in a vase, etc.

EXERCISE
Visualization for receiving specific forgiveness

Settle yourself in a comfortable, relaxed posture, close your eyes and breathe gently, concentrating your mind on the area immediately above and between the eyes. [pause]

When you are ready, picture in your mind the person from whom you wish to receive forgiveness (if this proves difficult, refer to a photograph). [pause]

When you have a strong image of this person, read out your letter to them and picture them receiving it in a loving, kindly way. [pause]

When you have finished reading out the letter, ask them to forgive you and allow yourself to feel that forgiveness flowing towards you and into your heart. Allow the forgiveness to spread through your body in a warm glow. [pause]

When you have received forgiveness, thank the person, wish them well, and make any gesture you feel is appropriate such as hugging, shaking hands, bowing, etc. [pause]

Then allow them to fade from your mind, sending them on

their way with love. Notice how much lighter you feel now that you have received forgiveness. [pause]

When you are ready, breathe a little more deeply, become aware of your surroundings once more, and open your eyes slowly.

EXERCISE
Visualization for receiving non-specific forgiveness

Settle yourself in a comfortable, relaxed posture, close your eyes and breathe gently, concentrating your mind on the area immediately above and between the eyes. [pause]

When you are ready, picture in front of you a bright, radiant white light which grows until it fills your mind, or until you can picture yourself stepping forward into the light. [pause]

Allow yourself to be enveloped in this light, which is all-loving and all-forgiving. Feel it spreading through your body in a warm glow, filling your heart with unconditional loving acceptance. Rest in its peace until you feel you have been totally forgiven. [pause]

Notice how much lighter you feel now that you have received forgiveness.

When you are ready, breathe a little more deeply and become aware of your surroundings. Once your attention is back in the room, open your eyes.

REFRAMING OR SETTING GOALS

You may find that some items on your list can be reframed into a positive statement, or into goals that need to be set.

EXERCISE

1. Write out your regret.
2. Reframe this into a positive statement or benefit.
3. If appropriate, create a goal and set a date for commencing.

Ensure that you have worked through all the items on your original lists.

CUTTING THE TIES WITH THE PAST

Our difficulties from the past are often, seemingly, inextricably linked to other people with whom we have become 'enmeshed' and with whom we have created bonds which are not always good for us. This is particularly true in 'love' relationships but can apply to any interaction with other people.

For the past seventeen years I have used a method of 'cutting the ties' which is closely linked to, but not based on, the work of Phyllis Krystal[4]. It involves letting go of all the 'oughts, shoulds, if onlies' which make our contact with people conditional and which hold us, and them, back from developing as people in our own right.

I have found this work to be particularly effective at times of crisis or change and it can be extremely relevant to the menopause as this is often a period of letting go of responsibilities for the family, or of moving away from the unspoken restrictions that your family placed on you. It can, of course, also be a time when husbands leave and parents die.

Cutting can be carried out with anyone regardless of whether they are still alive or active in your life (which makes it perfect for releasing parents, ex-husbands or lovers). The practice is also useful in releasing from addictive substances such as alcohol, nicotine, drugs or food. The Bach Remedies Walnut and Honeysuckle are helpful in cutting the ties and should be taken both prior to the cutting and for several weeks following.

As the visualization frees you from the past, and particularly from people who have been holding you back without your realizing it, it can be helpful to do a 'blank' cutting, creating the circle and then asking that whoever you most need to cut away from should appear in the circle. A participant on one of my workshops did this and was surprised to find a headmaster appear, for whom she had worked as a teacher. She realized that his sadistic cruelty and violence had deeply marked her and had affected her love of teaching since that time. Once she cut away from him, she was freed from his negative influence.

The work involves cutting the emotional ties that have

built up and sets both parties free to be themselves and to take their own place in life. *It does not cut off the love*, but it does remove all the conditions, the 'oughts, shoulds, buts and if onlies,' that can attach themselves to what masquerades as 'love'. For rather too many people, 'loving' their children or partner involves a subtle radiation of acceptance or non-acceptance based on whether the other person is conforming to what is required or considered to be 'good'. Love, unfortunately, is all too often a method of control. Paradoxically, in letting go, the bond of love often becomes stronger and the relationship improves as the other person is perceived as an individual in their own right. The imaging is also useful for working with people, such as parents or grandparents, whom you have loved very much but who have now passed on, as they can still be having a deep influence in your life and you may still be living out their hopes for you.

It has been suggested that this exercise may interfere with another person's autonomy and rights. However, the meadow in this visualization represents your own inner space. In doing this exercise, you are inviting another person to manifest in that inner space. They are there by your invitation, not by right (although they may well already occupy part of that space without your invitation, which interferes with your own autonomy). By using the circles you delineate the space which each of you can occupy while doing the work. You should not let the circles overlap, nor allow the other person to move into your circle. When the work is complete, you set them free and send them back to their own place. In other words, they move out of your inner space and into their own. Thus, you are each set free to inhabit your own autonomous space.

The meditation is set in a meadow but some people find it easier to picture the seashore, the side of a lake, or some other peaceful place. It is important to use your own images, rather than ones I impose on you, so adapt the wording if necessary. During the imaging work, the ties can manifest in many ways – nets, hooks, umbilical cords, etc. – and in many places. It is quite common to find a sexual tie linking you to a father or brother or even to your mother. These images are the subconscious mind's way of symbolically representing an emotional truth and should be accepted as such.

Part of the work involves removing the ties, the place where they have been on each person being healed and sealed with light, and the other part involves destroying these ties. I find the most useful way of doing this is to have a large fire, as again the symbolism is important. As the fire burns, it transmutes the tie into energy. It is also possible to use water to dissolve or wash away the ties. The one method I do not recommend is to bury them, as symbolically this does not free you from them, and they may well sprout and grow again. Having said that, I have learned from years of experience that it is impossible to be dogmatic as, just occasionally, a tie may be transformed through death and rebirth, of which the ritual of burying can be a part.

EXERCISE
Tie-cutting visualization

This visualization should be taped, leaving plenty of time to carry out the instructions, or be read aloud by a facilitator. The advantage of having a facilitator is that they can work to your pace, and suggest alternatives should you find the exercise difficult. You can repeat the exercise as many times as required according to how many people you wish to cut the ties with, and the exercise can be repeated daily for difficult cuttings until you feel it is complete. As with all imaging work, you only have to ask for what you need for it to be there, so the tools for the cutting will be available.

Begin by sitting in a comfortable chair, with your eyes closed. Breathe gently, relax and let go of any tension you may feel. Withdraw your attention from the outside world and into your self. Without opening your eyes, look at the spot above and between your eyebrows. [pause]

When you are ready, picture yourself in a meadow on a warm, sunny day. Really feel the grass underneath your feet and the warmth of the sun coming down onto your face, with a gentle breeze playing around you. Spend a little time exploring your meadow and then choose the spot where you want to do this work [pause]

Draw a circle on the ground around yourself as you stand in the meadow. The circle should be at arms length and go right around you. You can use paint, chalk, light or whatever comes to mind. This circle delineates your space. [pause]

In front of you, close to but not touching, draw another circle the same size. [pause]

Invite the person with whom you wish to cut the ties to step into the circle. (If you have difficulty in seeing the person clearly, you can picture a photograph being placed in the circle.) [pause]

Explain to the person why you are doing this exercise, tell them that you are not cutting off any unconditional love there may be, but that you wish to be free from the old emotional conditioning and bonds that built up in the past. [pause]

Look to see how the ties symbolically manifest themselves. [pause] Then spend time removing them, first from the other person and then from yourself, healing and sealing the places where they were with light. Make sure you get all the ties, especially the ones around the back which you may overlook. Pile the ties up outside the circle. [pause]

When you are sure you have cleared all the ties and sealed all the places where they have been, let unconditional love, forgiveness and acceptance (where possible) flow between you and the other person. [pause]

Then move the other person back to their own space; let them go to where they belong. [pause]

Gather up all the ties and find an appropriate way of destroying them. You may wish to have a large bonfire onto which you throw them, or a swiftly flowing river into which you cast them. Make sure you have destroyed all the ties. [pause]

If you are using a fire, move nearer to the flames and feel the transmuted energy warming, purifying, healing and energizing you; filling all the empty spaces left by removing the ties. Absorb as much of this energy as you need. If you feel able to, move into the fire and become like the phoenix, reborn from the flames.

If you are using water, you may like to enter the water, or to use the heat of the sun to purify, heal and energize yourself. [pause]

Repeat the cutting with another person if you wish. When you have completed all the cutting you wish to do, bring your attention back into the room and allow yourself plenty of time to readjust, breathing more deeply and bringing yourself into full awareness of sitting in the chair with your feet firmly on the ground. Open your eyes when ready.

RELEASING BAGGAGE FROM THE PAST

It is possible that you are carrying burdens and baggage from the past that are no longer appropriate but to which you have become so attached that you do not notice them. Sometimes the 'rubbish' breaks down into nice fertile compost out of which something new can grow; at other times it becomes a putrefying mass. It is this latter condition which blocks and drains our creative energy. The menopause is an extremely appropriate time to release this and to free the energies involved. The following visualization enables you to clear these burdens without having to identify them first.

The visualization should be taped, with appropriate pauses, or read by a facilitator who can follow your own timing.

EXERCISE

Settle yourself comfortably in a chair. Breathe gently and relax. Close your eyes and look at the spot above and between the eyebrows. [pause]

Picture yourself in a meadow on a nice, warm sunny day and really feel the grass underneath your feet and the warmth of the sun on your face. [pause]

Ask to be shown symbolically all the burdens and baggage you have been carrying from the past that you no longer need. Collect these together into a big pile, remembering to look under rocks and in other hidden places. You may find that you are carrying some of the baggage in your body and need to remove this and add it to the pile. [pause]

When you are sure you have collected everything, look at the pile and notice how much lighter you feel without the burden of the past. Then find an appropriate way to destroy the old baggage. You may like to use a large fire, or a swiftly flowing river. A hot air balloon can be useful to put living things or people into, cutting the rope when you are ready to let them go. Spend time disposing of your pile in an appropriate way and really enjoy the feeling of release this brings to you. [pause]

When you have completed the disposal, allow yourself to draw near to the fire (entering it if possible) or enter the water, and use the energy to purify and heal all the places where the burdens and baggage were held within you. [pause]

As you leave the fire or the water, become aware that you have been regenerated and reborn, light and pure. Be aware of the energy that flows within you and the possibilities that are open before you. [pause]

When you are ready, return your awareness to the room, noticing how much lighter and freer your body feels as you become aware of it again. When you are ready, open your eyes.

THE MOURNING RITE

You are now ready to carry out the mourning rite. You may like to burn scented candles or incense and play a piece of sombre music or one of the tapes specially written to create a ceremonial atmosphere. The lights should be dimmed slightly and you may find it appropriate to wrap yourself in a cloak or to wear a colour which you particularly associate with mourning.

Gather together your list of things to be mourned, any letters or photographs you feel it is appropriate to refer to or to burn, a box of tissues, a large ashtray (or use a fireplace if you have one), and a candle to light at the appropriate time. Choose a place in the room which feels right for you and settle yourself comfortably.

EXERCISE

When you are ready to begin, remind yourself that you are here to mourn the past, to acknowledge the feelings attached to that past, and then to let go of the past. Read out loud each item on your list, allowing time to honour and express the feelings attached, and making any gestures such as dancing, chanting, painting, re-reading letters, looking at photographs, burning the letters, etc., which feel right for you. Do not be afraid to cry or to feel anger if this is appropriate and stay with the emotion until it passes. If you are allowing yourself to fully feel the emotions they may well be intense but will not last long. Repeat this for each item on your list.

When you have finished reading the list, burn it ceremonially, saying out loud, 'I have mourned the past and I now relinquish it and its hold on the present'. Watch the smoke from the list curling away and allow the past to dissolve. Sit quietly, feeling the burden of the past and all your regrets slipping away. Forgive yourself, if necessary, for allowing those regrets to arise.

Do not hurry the process but when you have allowed sufficient time for the mourning, change the music to something joyous and uplifting, turn up the lights and throw off the mourning clothes, replacing them with a bright colour to symbolize your new freedom. Then light the candle and by its light, read your list of reframed benefits, and review the goals you set, allowing yourself to look forward with joy and expectation to the new present you have created. You may feel that you need to dance, sing, paint or find some other way to express your joy. Stay with this feeling for as long as possible, perhaps preparing a celebration meal as a way of ending the rite and carrying the new energy into your everyday life.

5. ❖ *Female Sexuality*

Sexuality is meant to be an all-pervasive energizing force and not just a genital focus.[1]

Barbara Hand Clow

WHAT IS SEXUALITY?

Sexuality is far more than the act of sexual intercourse. It has to do with feelings and sensuality; with eroticism and lust; with fantasy and self-expression; with intimacy and sharing, and with sexual orientation. It can be passive or aggressive, overt or covert. It is a complex emotional response to life based on the urge towards caring and nurturing, tenderness and receptivity, and yet cannot be separated from the will to power and the urge to dominate and control. The feminine energy is the gentle, passive and accepting yin force of the cosmos. Nevertheless, female sexuality embraces and incorporates its counterpart, the active and outgoing yang energy. Our own personal and unique sexuality, with its particular inner mix of masculine and feminine, is inherent in how we present ourselves to the world. It is expressed through body language and subtle gesture. Sexuality is a powerful, magical urge towards self-expression that demands to be integrated into the totality of female experience and is a celebration of life itself.

There are as many images of female sexuality as there are individual women, but the stereotype roles include the eternal girl and the perpetual mother; the flirt, the wife and the mistress; the career woman or the courtesan; the man-eater and the man-hater; the ministering angel; the bitch and the bimbo; the witch and the Wise Woman, all of which interweave and change according to how, and by whom, the woman is perceived. These roles are often portrayed through body language and dress. The eternal girl is frilly, with bows in her hair; the perpetual mother is flowing and earthy, or matronly and neat; whilst the flirt is provocative and the career woman uses power-dressing to convey her status. Dress may be used to disguise sexuality, or to cover up and compensate for a lack of sexuality or to portray an ideal, as in the advertising industry.

For many women, sexuality is inextricably linked to their role as mother (a role which may be biological or surrogate – as in the case of the woman who 'mothers' her partner, clients or charges, etc.). This link between sexuality and mothering is not just a question of mental attitude; it is a physical sensation. Childbirth and breastfeeding can be powerfully erotic experiences, and contact with the child may provide what the partner cannot. A woman whose husband was killed when her baby was six months old continued to breastfeed her child until he went to school, gaining considerable sexual and emotional satisfaction in the process.

The urge to nurture is deeply embedded in the feminine psyche. Mrs Thatcher, that epitome of the ruthless career woman, was nevertheless said to insist on cooking her current favourite political colleague scrambled eggs whenever he came to call at No. 10. When taken to extremes this deeply instinctual urge to be mother becomes the woman's total expression of sexuality, creating a life crisis when the biological function ceases or the children move away – leaving a mother suffering from the 'empty nest' syndrome in their wake. Such a woman urgently needs to explore the full potential of her sexuality as an antidote to the crisis, and to own her power as a woman.

Owning sexuality has to do with honouring the feminine principle within oneself and acknowledging the complementary, masculine, one, allowing each the appropriate space for expression. It is concerned with being centred in one's own femininity as a source of being and with utilizing sexual energy as a creative resource as well as the source of sexual activity. And, if you ever doubt that woman is meant to be sexual, remember that she alone of all God's, or rather the Goddess's, creatures has an organ exclusively devoted to sexual pleasure – the clitoris. This fact is, for me, the greatest argument against the concept of a male god and the sanctity of celibacy. I firmly believe that

woman was meant to be sexual. I equally firmly believe
that there is no 'right' or 'wrong' expression of sexuality
and this chapter is intended for heterosexual and lesbian
woman as similar issues arise for both at menopause.

Women's sexual experience during the menopausal rite
of passage is important to their well-being, as women who
are in a fulfilling relationship are less likely to experience a
loss of identity, and those who use their sexual energy
creatively will have a much richer total life experience. It
has been suggested[2] that the women who experience most
difficulty with menopausal symptoms are those who are
not comfortable with their own female nature or those
whose identity is so deeply rooted in their reproductive
system that they cannot imagine life beyond that function;
and those for whom the outer mask of an attractive face
and body represents their desirability and value in the inner,
as well as the outer, world.

If self-esteem is indissolubly tied to physical attractiveness
or biological function, then inevitably, when that attribute
undergoes drastic change, an identity crisis will result.
Unfortunately, our society sees sex appeal as the prerogative
of the younger woman, and women who have progressed
into middle age are expected to become asexual beings –
despite the fact that they have at least twenty five years of
potential sexual activity in front of them.

Some women, particularly those from a religious background, may have been inculcated with the view that sex
is only for procreation, and therefore feel extremely guilty
when they continue to have sexual needs after their fertility
has waned. Women who do express their sexual needs are
frequently seen, in Britain at least, as 'disgusting' or 'not
acting their age', particularly if it is combined with 'cradle
snatching' a 'toy boy'; whereas men, in the same circumstances, are applauded for their virility. There are signs that
this 'sexually invisible' attitude towards women is slowly
changing, but it is women themselves who have to make
the shift into enjoying, rather than apologizing for, their
continued sexuality.

Other women, the 'new' women who have learned to
demand that their needs be met, may be so busy chasing
an orgasm that they are missing out on intimacy. Less

assertive women may be so afraid of losing the 'love' of their partner that they never pay any attention to their own needs, allowing the sexual rhythm of the other to dominate. During the 1980s, the discovery by women's magazines of orgasm as a fertile source of articles put tremendous pressure on women, who felt deprived and inadequate if they did not have an orgasm every time they had sexual contact.

For many women the menopause coincides with loss of a sexual partner: partners may die or prop up their own diminishing sexual peer-status by pursuing a younger woman – seeking the spurious reassurance of sexual attraction. Divorce is common. The woman herself may realize that her relationship is stultified and unsatisfactory, and decide to leave so that she is then free to explore her sexuality in a more fulfilling way.

Women who do remain in their relationship may well find that diminishing sexual activity is more related to problems with their relationship than with their own level of sexual desire and is therefore a separate issue from their continuing sexuality. Indeed, studies have shown that most women experience a loss of desire before rather than during the menopause[3] although the problem of vaginal dryness, with its associated discomfort, can affect the capacity for pleasure. This is, however, easily remedied by the use of a vaginal lubricant (available over the counter from pharmacies) or by a medically prescribed hormone cream. For many women, being freed from the need for contraception opens up a new sexual spontaneity in the post-menopause phase and offers a creative form of self-expression.

If you have worked through Chapters 3 and 4, you may well have uncovered some of your attitudes towards sex and sexuality, but the exercise below will give you further valuable information to work with.

EXERCISE
Your attitude to sexuality

1. How do you feel about being a woman?
2. Do you believe that sexuality and sex are necessarily the same thing?

3. Do you believe that physical attractiveness is a necessary part of sexual attraction?
4. Do you believe that sexuality is tied to your reproductive function?
5. Do you believe you are only complete when you have a sexual partner?
6. Do you believe that a woman's role should be as the passive partner?
7. Is your sex life dominated by another person?
8. Are you satisfied with your sex life? If no, how would you improve it?
9. Are you able to enjoy your sexuality without necessarily needing sexual contact?
10. Do fantasy and sensuality have a place in your life?
11. Would you like to explore a different facet of your sexuality but have been afraid to do so? If yes, which facet(s)?
12. What is holding you back?
13. What do you believe about sex and sexuality in middle age?
14. Are there any negative statements above which could be reframed into positive statements or affirmations? Don't forget to practise your affirmations regularly.
15. List as many ways as possible for expressing your sexuality. Try them out!

THE PERSONAL PRUDE

Most of us carry within us a voice that is a compilation of parental messages about sex, previous experience, things that people have said, etc. This voice can intervene at the most inauspicious moments with criticism or comments that can totally ruin our sex life and destroy our sexual confidence. A friend has a voice that always said 'Shhh..' just at the crucial moment. Anne Dickson[+] calls this voice 'the personal prude' and I have adapted the exercise below from her work.

Once the personal prude has been identified, it is possible to disentangle oneself from the messages it gives. For example, a woman had a 'puritanical father' as a personal prude. She fantasized her father smilingly handing her over to her lover, blessing the union.

The following exercise can either be taped, with appropriate pauses, or memorized. You may like to choose a house in which you lived as a child, or to find a fantasy house to explore. Do not try to force the images or answers to come; allow them to arise spontaneously in your mind. Have a pen and paper handy so that you can jot down the answers.

EXERCISE
Meeting the personal prude

Settle yourself comfortably in a chair or in bed. Close your eyes and breathe gently for a while until you feel relaxed and comfortable. [pause]

Then picture yourself standing in front of a house. [pause] When you feel ready, open the front door and go into the house. Immediately in front of you you will see a flight of stairs leading up to the bedrooms. Your personal prude is waiting to meet you in one of these rooms, so make your way up the stairs and look in all the bedrooms until you find the figure you are seeking. [pause]

Enter this room and look carefully at the figure. Does it remind you of anyone you know? Spend time becoming familiar with this figure. [pause] Then ask this figure to repeat to you the messages it brings. If necessary, picture yourself making love and listen to the voice of the prude standing by your bed. [pause]

Now, try to negotiate a new policy with your prude. Explain that you are trying to create a new image for yourself as a sexual being. Picture the prude looking on joyfully while you enjoy all facets of your sexuality. Ask the prude to give you some positive messages to affirm your sexual persona. [pause]

Ask your personal prude what new name would be suitable for it to match this new attitude. [pause]

Then thank the figure for coming to you and slowly return your attention to the room. When you are ready, open your eyes and note down the answers you received.

1. Who was your personal prude?
2. What were the old messages your personal prude gave?
3. What were the new messages? Can you transform any of these into affirmations?
4. What was the new name of your personal prude?

EXPLORING YOUR BODY

For most women growing up during the 1940s and 1950s, the body was a 'no-go area' and sex education was restricted to the minimum. Even the onset of the Swinging Sixties failed to liberate the body despite the changing pattern of sexual activity created by the spurious freedom of 'the pill' (an invention which in many ways took away women's attunement to, and control over, their own bodily processes).

Women from this era often have a poor body image coupled with a body awareness that is a nebulous collection of myths, 'old wives tales' and media hype, supplemented with memories of furtive teenage fumbling and somewhat routine sexual contact later on – unless they were fortunate enough to find a good lover at an early stage in their sexual exploration. The promiscuity of the Swinging Sixties in a way hindered women as a wide variety of sexual partners does not necessarily guarantee sexual fulfilment; and, in any case, many women now entering menopause were married at a young age and missed the change in sexual standards by a few years.

Consequently, few women now reaching the menopause really know and understand their body, and even fewer are aware of how their emotions affect their body's functioning. Many women are still controlled by parental messages about 'no touching' and pleasurable experience of the body may be severely affected by old taboos.

If your sexuality and attitude to your body are still confused by ignorance or controlled by 'the personal prude', you can take the time to explore your body, to learn to love it, and begin to understand how it responds to stimulation and becomes sexually aroused.

EXERCISE

Choose a time when you will be undisturbed for at least an hour, and if possible lock the door to ensure privacy and to give a feeling of safety. Make sure that the room is comfortably warm and sufficiently well lit (candles give a soft and flattering light). You may like to burn perfumed oil or incense and to play some of your favourite music to help you relax. You will need a full-length and a hand mirror, some coloured pencils and paper. A bath or shower beforehand can help you to relax and feel good.

When you are feeling happy and relaxed, begin to take off your clothes and spend some time enjoying the freedom of being naked. You might like to dance or to move around the room so that you can feel the warm air playing sensuously on your skin. You may find it comfortable to lie on a sheepskin rug and enjoy its softness. Give yourself at least ten or fifteen minutes of pleasurable enjoyment. You may like to massage oil or moisturizer into your body, attuning to its sensual feel. Or to gently stroke and explore your skin to see how it responds to touch. Do whatever feels good to you. Don't be afraid to experiment; you may like firm strokes, or light gentle circular movements.

Then, when you are feeling completely relaxed and good about your body, stand in front of a full-length mirror and really look at yourself for another ten or fifteen minutes. Usually we tend to have a longish look at our face and hair and rarely, if ever, give our naked body more than a quick glance. This time, however, linger on your body. Notice where it curves, how rounded it is, recognize the different textures and colours of your skin, and explore all its little hollows and hidden places. Notice how much space it takes up; many women have a false body image they have carried around for years. (If you feel there is a discrepancy between what you see and how much space you feel you take up, ask someone to draw round you – at a later date – and fill in measurements, shape, etc., until you become more familiar with your actual body size.)

Notice how you feel as you look at your body: are you tense, curious, surprised, inhibited, pleased, shy, sad? Can you look at yourself face-on or do you tend to turn away and look sideways? Are you inhibited by old taboos?

See which parts of your body you feel most comfortable with, which bits you are judging harshly. Given the diet and glamour mentality of the modern world, most women feel that their body isn't good enough in some way. We are used to critically, rather than lovingly, assessing our body. This time, pay loving attention to your body. It's yours, you live in it, this is home, so pay special attention to any parts you may have been neglecting or condemning. Look at it from all angles, see how the fall of light alters how it appears. You may like to take the time to sketch or draw your body in a favourite pose. If any issues come up for you, then take the time to write in your journal and explore exactly where they are coming from and the associations you have with different parts of your body.

Now move into a more intimate exploration of your body. Sit comfortably on the bed or in a big chair so that you can tuck your feet up by your buttocks and open up your knees. You are now in an ideal position to explore the part of your body that isn't usually on view – your genital region. You will probably need a hand mirror to see clearly. This part of yourself is as unique as every other part, and you are not here to make comparisons or wonder if you are normal. There are infinite varieties of shape and colour, just as there are with bodies. Spend at least ten or fifteen minutes simply looking and accepting what you see.

It can be a powerful experience to name what you are looking at, either with its correct anatomical name or a pet name. Many women are a little vague about the precise location of various parts, so a map is included here to guide you. Spend some time exploring this hidden part of yourself and remember that it's OK to touch! Don't forget that the vagina has an inside as well as an

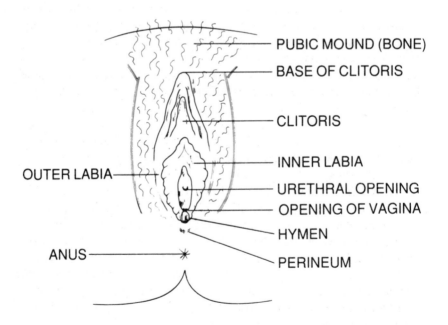

Fig. 9   Genital map

outside although, unless you have a speculum, you will have to explore this by touch alone.

When you have finished your exploration, make your own map. This can be a pencil sketch or a full colour portrait. It doesn't matter whether you can draw or not as, unless you choose otherwise, you are the only one who is going to see the finished result, although some women find great enjoyment and acceptance in displaying their self-portrait. Then spend some time exploring your feelings in your journal.

You may then like to continue the exploration of your body with a partner, teaching this partner what you enjoy and trying out new types of touch. You may also enjoy have a professional massage to help you move further into your body, especially as the body holds many emotional tensions that can be released by massage. Or, you could find a friend who is willing to help you experiment with touch and sensation. This kind of contact between friends builds up trust and self-confidence for moving into sexual contacts with a partner at a later date.

Massage is also excellent for couples; giving each other pleasure is both a bonding and a delight. If you wish to set the boundary of allowing massage only, then say so. Many women find they can enjoy their sensuality more if the pressure of sexuality is taken away. If you are willing for it to lead on to other things, then allow this to take its course quite naturally.

You may also like to extend the exploration and valuing of your body through working as a couple. You make statements about your body, and your partner simply mirrors them back to you (avoiding any hint of criticism). So, if you feel you have 'saggy boobs', your partner will say: 'I'm hearing you say that you have saggy boobs', or more simply, 'You feel you have saggy boobs'. On the other hand, if you feel you have great breasts, your partner will affirm this in you. In this way you are honouring your feelings about your body and may well come to learn to enjoy it more openly when you have voiced your deepest criticisms and compliments.

If you feel able to accept feedback from your partner, you might well find out that those 'saggy boobs' are in fact perceived as one of your most alluring features. What must be avoided at all costs is getting into a 'Oh no I don't/Oh yes you do' type argument which would cause you to devalue your body again. The aim is to help you accept, and value, your body and to feel comfortable inhabiting it.

LOVING YOURSELF

Many women now entering the menopause were brought up before the 'Me Generation' came into being, certainly before children were seen as anything other than an extension of their parents. As children, we usually had to 'be seen and not heard'. Behaviour was confused with the child. Comments such as: 'You are so naughty, . . greedy, . . rude, . . thoughtless, . . selfish', and suchlike instilled in us a sense that we *were* the way in which we behaved. In addition, we were taught to believe that it was other people, and particularly other people's needs, who counted – particularly true for the generation of war babies in Britain who grew up with shortages and sacrifice.

The most important thing we lacked was the ability to love ourselves. And, if we cannot love ourselves, then we most certainly cannot love another person. Loving yourself does not mean being arrogant, selfish, self-centred or any of the other things we fear are 'not nice'. It means liking 'Me', valuing yourself warts and all, being non-judgemental, caring and nurturing yourself, acknowledging strengths and weaknesses, being self-sufficient and having a strong sense of self. This enables us to put ourselves first and meet our own needs without feeling guilty. It means finding that all those things we looked for in another person in order to feel complete are actually within us.

So remember, the menopause can be a time when you learn to love yourself for the first time. If you find yourself alone during this transition, take the opportunity to do all those things you have been promising yourself instead of sitting around waiting for someone else to make it happen. Being alone is different from being lonely, and if you love yourself, and therefore enjoy your own company, it will not be a problem.

EXERCISE

1. Think of as many ways as possible to pamper yourself, and do them. The little things are important, like taking the time to have a scented bath or a massage, giving yourself a flower or one single, luscious handmade chocolate.
2. Make time for yourself, even if it is only half an hour a day and enjoy it without feeling guilty.
3. In your journal, list all the nice qualities about yourself – we are so used to looking at, or being told about, our faults that we forget the good things. Post up lists around the house to remind you.
4. Don't forget to fill in your 'Bouquets for Ruth' (see Chapter 3).
5. Try to speak to someone new each day, even if it has to be the girl on the check-out till.

One of the best ways of showing yourself that you love yourself is to give yourself pleasure, and one of the best ways to do this is with masturbation.

THERAPEUTIC MASTURBATION

This next exercise was taught to me by a very old lady who always looked on it as a way of self-expression and of generating a very special kind of energy. It can be a very powerful, and empowering, experience and it is a useful way of exploring your sexual response, learning what stimulates you and the kind of touch you enjoy.

If you are able to release your own sexual tension, it takes the pressure off your partner (assuming you have one) to 'perform', and it can prevent the kind of casual sexual contact which arises out of need but somehow feels unsatisfactory afterwards. Some women do find it a lonely activity, which heightens their sense of being separate and, possibly, unloved. It is, however, a way of loving oneself. It is also a wonderful opportunity to indulge in erotic fantasy and to exercise your creative imagination.

Masturbation has the added advantage of keeping the vagina lubricated, an important point if the elasticity of the vaginal lining is to be maintained. Hormonal changes can 'dry out' the vagina and regular sexual activity has been shown to help prevent this. And, as Anne Dickson points out: '[masturbation] comes highly recommended as a remedy for insomnia, menstrual pain, headaches, fatigue and backache.⁵' Nevertheless, as Anne Dickson also points out, 'The importance of masturbation is the quality of time spent with oneself', so if you are uncertain about your attitude to pleasuring yourself it can be useful to clarify how you feel before you start.

EXERCISE

1.   Write down everything you think and feel about masturbation, all the parental messages, your previous experiences, etc.
2.   Are any of these thoughts and feelings going to prevent you from enjoying masturbation?
3.   If yes, can you reframe the negative 'taboo' aspect into a positive permission for self-expression of your sexuality?

You are now ready to begin a pleasurable experience of self-exploration. As the purpose of this experience is to put you in touch with your own energies, and help you to harness them, it is not appropriate to share it with another person, so ensure that your privacy will not be disturbed. You may like to use music, incense, perfume, fantasy, sex toys, etc., to set the scene. Decide whether you will feel more comfortable with a low light or no light at all (some women find it adds to their enjoyment to be able to watch themselves in a mirror).

EXERCISE

Begin by stimulating yourself in whatever way you find most pleasurable, experimenting with touch and using any aids you may find helpful (a vibrator can be useful in the initial stages but you need the sensitivity of your fingers for the final part). Take your time and allow yourself to almost reach orgasm two or three times but stop before you do.

Then rest your hand against the pubic mound so that the base of your middle finger lies at the base of the clitoris and the finger curves down over the clitoris and into your vagina. Begin by using the tip of your middle finger to stimulate the vagina until orgasm is just starting, then gradually move the stimulation down your finger until you reach the base of the clitoris and, *at the same time*, feel the energy of the orgasm moving into the base of the spine and then up the spine as you change the pressure of your finger. Eventually you will be able to move the energy right up into the top of the head and energy will then flood through your body in waves. Breathe out in time with these waves allowing the energy to reach right down to your fingers and toes, and as you breathe in imagine the energy circulating around your body and returning to its source at the base of the spine.

With a little practice, the circulation of the energy becomes automatic and the orgasm becomes a whole body experience which leaves you feeling revitalized and glowing. As your awareness deepens, you will begin to contact the magical, spiritual level of being which is totally creative and free. The masturbation then becomes a meditation which connects you to the creative energies of the cosmos.

UNBLOCKING SEXUAL ENERGY

If you have been holding back your sexual energy for any reason, you may find that it is locked into your body and held around the base of your spine or bouncing around in your head, creating a headache. A simple exercise will help you to free this energy and release it for your enjoyment. (It may also release other emotions such as anger which have been locked in. If these arise, then spend time expressing them in your diary and return to the exercises in Chapter 4.)

EXERCISE

Close your eyes and imagine that you are trying to keep a hula-hoop turning around your hips. Picture how your hips move in a wide circle. Now stand with your feet placed directly under your hips. Slowly move your hips with a wide circular movement; going to the right, out to the front, to the left and then out to the back. Repeat this circle ten times, and then change direction and repeat ten times more.

This exercise should be practised night and morning for at least two weeks until the sexual energy begins to flow. Once the benefits are established, you may well wish to carry on as part of your daily routine.

As an aside, I often wonder whether there is a direct link between the hula-hoop craze of the 1950s and the sexual liberation of the Swinging Sixties. Did a generation of hip-swinging young women prevent the locking up of their adolescent energies and thereby pave the way for sexual freedom?

CIRCULATING SEXUAL ENERGY

I first came across the following exercise in a women's magazine about thirty years ago. It was also taught by the same elderly lady from whom I learned the therapeutic masturbation. I have since learnt that it is very ancient indeed, having been taught in pharaonic Egypt, India and China, and quite probably in many other cultures as well. It not only circulates the sexual energy throughout the body, energizing the chakras (major energy centres located up the spine and in the head) and major organs of the body, but also transmutes the basic biological sexual urge into creative energy that can be tapped for other purposes.

When first practising this exercise, it can be useful to choose a time when you are feeling sexually aroused but unable or unwilling to do anything about the arousal, or when you have finished making love but still have sexual energy available. You can practise in public without anyone being the wiser, so it is ideal for car or train journeys. After a while, it will become second nature to attune to the sexual energy without having to wait for arousal. The energy is usually felt in the genital area at first, but after practice it begins at the base of the spine and the exercise can then start from this point.

EXERCISE

If you wish to build up your energy before practising, lie down for about twenty minutes and gently breathe into a point an inch or two below your navel. (Focus your attention on that particular spot and imagine the breath going in and out through your skin rather than your lungs.) Your belly should rise and fall with your breathing and you will feel yourself become very centred and still around this point. The point will most probably get quite hot and will feel greatly energized.

EXERCISE
The micro-cosmic orbit

Sit in an upright position, or lie flat on your back, and close your eyes to aid concentration. Take your attention down to the perineum (the point between the vagina and the anus; see the map on p. 128) and slightly contract this point. Feel the sexual energy begin to flow from this point, and guide it upwards past the anus to the base of the spine. Then allow your attention to move up the spine, taking the energy with it. It will pass from the base of the spine, up to the waist, behind the solar plexus and the heart, and into the neck, and then up the back of the head into the crown.

The energy will then begin to travel back down the front of the body, passing over the face, down into the throat, over the heart and the solar plexus, past the uterus and back down to the perineum where it begins the circuit once again. (The Chinese method suggests that the tongue is placed lightly against the roof of the mouth behind the teeth so that it forms a bridge for the energy to flow down.) Continue to practise for a few minutes, gradually building up the time spent as you become more accustomed to the energy flow.

The Chinese method[6] finishes by spiralling the energy into the navel, where it is stored until required. When I first learnt the practice, it was suggested that the energy should be left to circulate until required, or allowed to flow out of the body through the feet if it was too strong. It is worth experimenting to see which is most comfortable for you. (If the energy is too strong it can cause a headache to develop, in which case visualize pushing the energy out through your feet to release it.)

TONING EXERCISE FOR THE VAGINA AND BLADDER

Another exercise which can be carried out discreetly is that of toning the vaginal muscles. Again, this is a very ancient practice. Women in the Orient were said to have been taught it to pleasure their husbands beyond measure, but it has a prosaic benefit in that it can also strengthen the pelvic floor, thus avoiding prolapse, and prevent incontinence from developing – an important benefit as the hormonal changes which dry and thin the vaginal lining can also weaken the entrance to the bladder.

The exercise can be practised while sitting on the loo at first and then carried out at any convenient moment during the day. When you become really skilful it is possible to massage a penis from end to end simply by using the vaginal muscles.

EXERCISE

Rhythmically contract and release the muscles of the vagina, holding for a few seconds before letting go (the best way to develop this skill is to practise cutting off the flow of urine for a few moments by contracting your muscles in midstream). With a little practice, it is possible to contract the muscles at the front of the genital region, and then contract those around the anus, in order to control different parts of the vagina.

FOCUSING ON ORGASMIC FEELINGS

Research has shown that women who believe themselves to be unable to reach orgasm rarely have any physical cause for the inability. The cause usually lies in the mind and the control it has over the body. It is surprising how many 'inorgasmic' women suddenly learn how to have an orgasm when they are with a different lover or when they take a romantic second honeymoon. Menopausal women do seem to need more stimulation, and if you took twenty minutes to be aroused in your thirties, you may need to allow thirty to forty minutes build-up in your late forties to fifties.

If an inorgasmic woman can learn to switch her mind off and concentrate on the sexual feelings leading up to orgasm, then she is much more likely to experience the pleasure of sexual contact and to be able to express that pleasure as orgasm. This ability can be developed, either alone through masturbation or with the help of a sensitive partner. It is important that, initially, the arousal is carried out solely for the pleasure it brings, not for any resultant sexual contact. While your body is being stroked, mass-aged, kissed, nibbled or whatever else turns you on, you should concentrate your attention on the part being stimu-lated and the feelings that are aroused. Any thoughts that pass through your mind should be firmly ignored – no matter how pressing next week's laundry might seem at the time.

When you have had sufficient practice to recognize the moment of approaching orgasm, you can begin to include sexual contact with your partner in the experience, always keeping your attention on the site of the pleasure you receive. If you find your mind wandering, ask your partner to return to pleasuring you in whatever way you found most effective until you are again able to resume inter-course.

EXPRESSING FEELINGS

Now that your body is ready to join in the expression of your sexuality you may find that you have to pay attention to certain emotions that are arising. Or you may realize that, whilst you have had a surfeit of sensation, your body has been starved of, or cut off from feeling. This can mani-fest as a curious numbness, an absence of feeling; or a sudden surge of emotion which threatens to overwhelm.

The problem is that, through our past experience, we have become fragmented. Because we do what we think is correct, rather than what we instinctively feel is right, our heads have become cut off from our hearts. Because we have not learnt to recognize and express our feelings, our mind is separate from our body. We rarely recognize when emotions are affecting our body, and still less do we recog-nize that these emotions actually arise within our body. However they are quite literally, how we feel. If we cannot express these feelings, then they will create physical or emotional scars which affect the expression of our sexuality.

Fear can be one of the most paralysing of emotions, and one of the great difficulties facing many women is that of being too afraid to let go. Rigidly controlled by a fear of being out of control, a woman may be unable to give herself up to the sensations of orgasm. As one woman put it: 'It is not a question of not trusting him, I don't trust myself. I simply have to be in control of myself at all times'. As fear is usually a learned response, it can be reprogrammed.

If you make a point of noticing your body sensations when you are afraid, you will find that you tend to hold your breath, which comes in small, shallow gasps, and to pull yourself back slightly. Therefore, the easiest way to overcome fear, is to practise breathing! 'Correct' breathing is rhythmical and unhurried, coming from movements of the abdomen. As you breathe in, the belly expands and air is sucked deep into your lungs. As you breathe out, the belly contracts, forcing all the stale air out. A small pause between the movements increases the sense of natural and relaxed flow.

By working on your breathing during masturbation, it is possible to breathe out the fear and breathe in the pleasure, gradually allowing yourself to experience more and more of the sensations each time. A few good deep breaths as the moment of orgasm approaches will carry you over the threshold. You will then have moved out of your head and into your body. Once you have experienced this, and learned to trust yourself, then you can gently work through the same process with your partner. (It helps, of course, if you can trust your partner enough to communicate the fear and your need to overcome this. If you cannot, then perhaps this may be an area of your life in which a change is needed.)

Typical emotions which become inextricably interwoven with sexual responses are pain and anger, joy and sadness, anxiety and guilt. You may well have discovered some of these when working through earlier chapters, and hopefully will have released from their hold. Many of these emotions arise out of old physical or emotional abuse or coercion, some of which may be subtle and unrecognized. Several women I have spoken to have expressed their surprise, and immense anger, at realizing that they were abused within their marriages by husbands who demanded submission to their sexual needs. This can become an ongoing pattern which obscures and distorts a woman's real needs, and the emotions that are waiting to be expressed.

Learning to listen to your body and attuning to its needs are the first steps to overcoming this. The second is trusting yourself, and your partner, sufficiently to express those needs and find a way to meet them. Far too many people, men and women, expect their partner to know (presumably by telepathy) what they need and enjoy. Clearly stating the needs and asking for what is pleasurable can greatly enhance your sexual enjoyment – and you may find it helpful at this stage to return to Chapter 4 and review the section on learning to state your needs clearly.

Spending a few minutes quietly communing with your body before taking any action will help you to know what it is you really need. Sometimes the answer can surprise you, particularly if you have been using sex to keep down emotions that you didn't want to acknowledge. However, if emotions are dealt with as they arise, they do not have the opportunity to fester and become toxic, ultimately affecting the body, and thus many 'diseases' can be prevented. By moving more deeply into your feelings you are also able to express more joy and receive more pleasure in all aspects of your life. The passage through the menopause is, therefore, greatly enhanced by a free flow of feelings.

DEVELOPING INTIMACY

Many of us have never had the opportunity to develop intimacy with another person. Dysfunctional families, emotionally deprived childhoods, poor role models, previous bad experiences, and emotional inhibition on the part of our partners can all block intimacy and prevent us from coming close to another person. Genuine intimacy is about allowing another person to know us fully, and in return meeting that other person openly, holding nothing back. It is about trust and honesty, openness and acceptance; it is not symbiosis or dependency. It is the meeting point of two souls in authentic feeling experience. Intimacy is something that has to be experienced; it cannot be intellectualized but, just like any other relationship skill, it can be learned.

The following exercise develops intimacy and allows our partner to enter our own personal space, just as we enter theirs. Both parties must be willing to open to the other person. Choose a time when you will not be disturbed and set the scene by lowering the lights and maybe lighting a candle or incense.

You will need to sit facing each other, preferably cross-legged, with your knees touching each other. You can use the floor but may find it more comfortable to sit on the bed or on a large sofa. You can use cushions as a backrest if required.

EXERCISE

When you are ready to begin, bend your arms up and join hands palm to palm with the other person, right palm to your partner's left palm and vice versa. Choose a height that can be comfortably maintained (if at any time you feel strain on your arms, hold the position for just a few minutes more and you will usually find the pain goes away and you can continue). Look deeply into each other's eyes, allowing the eyes to blink naturally when necessary. Continue for at least fifteen minutes but preferably longer. Do not hold anything back; move your awareness out to meet the other person, open to them and allow them to know you fully, just as you will know them.

When you have finished, share your perceptions and your experience with your partner, remembering to listen effectively to their response. If you wish to, move naturally into making love.

THE LEGACY OF ABUSE

Although sexual abuse is finally being brought out into the open, it is still one of the most difficult areas for a woman to talk about, and one of the greatest problems can be in identifying whether or not she was actually abused. I have lost count of the number of women who, over the last seventeen years, have said to me, 'I think I was abused, although I cannot remember any specific incidents'. This is not surprising as sexual abuse is always treated as a deep, dark secret and the recipient is usually threatened with what will happen 'if they tell'. Add to this the experience of many children who have tried to tell a grown-up, only to have their story disbelieved as the abuser is usually a trusted friend or member of the family, and it is no wonder that the child quickly learns to deny what is happening and to screen off all conscious memory. We cannot remember because we cannot bear to remember; the pain is literally too great to be borne. So the mind takes action and erases the memory.

However, in the deepest recesses of our psyche *we know* what has happened and we live with the legacy of that abuse. Lack of trust, low self-esteem and lack of confidence, inability to be intimate, denial of our own feelings and a deep suspicion about other people's motives for being nice to us are only some of the long-term effects that even the mildest of abuse can have.

And this is one of the most important points: it does not need to have involved penetration by a male penis in order to have been abuse. Whilst some abuse is overtly sexual, 'flashing' or oral sex for instance, other abuse is very subtle. The father who comments suggestively on his teenage daughter's developing figure or who insists on entering the bathroom; the mother who washes her child's genitals rather too much or rather too carefully, or the friend's mother who baths the girls way past an appropriate age; the 'sex education' which insists that the body is dirty and men are only after one thing; the avuncular figure who forces kisses and fondling on an unwilling victim. All of these convey a covert feeling of 'wrongness' about a young girl's burgeoning sexuality, as does a house where sex is never mentioned, the television is switched off if anything sexual is shown, books are censored, and so forth. This is just as abusive as the household where porn films are openly available to young children.

In other households the abuse is emotional. There can be isolation, aggression or a symbiotic, dependent relationship between child and overprotective parent which allows no space and no separation, and which causes endless problems when that child is old enough to date.

In my own experiences, I can clearly remember the walk to school across fields and the succession of dirty old men in raincoats who would step out from the hedge and expose themselves; and then the sweetshop where the 'nice man' would offer you 'a feel and a sweetie', and the trusted family member who grabbed my developing eleven-year-old breasts and told me how nice they were. As I lived in a home where sex was 'not nice' and such things were never mentioned, it never occurred to me to tell my parents as I was sure I would be the one who would be punished. Friends who had similar experiences felt the same; those who endured penetrative abuse were told that they would be punished if someone found out. This is one of the fundamental problems of abuse. The child feels that it must be her fault, she must be doing something wrong.

This sense of wrongness then pervades the woman's whole attitude to sexuality. There is no pleasure in her body, sexual characteristics are something to be ashamed of, as is sexual contact. She is frightened to fully know herself as a woman and to let others know her in turn. She will often enter an abusive relationship – overt or covert – and repeat the pattern of her childhood. When the abuse has been great, she is often confused as to what 'love' really is and may equate violence with caring.

HEALING OLD ABUSE

The menopause tends to be a time when this old, unfinished business surfaces again. It is as though the psyche gives us an opportunity to free ourselves. That the past can be healed is a most important message for women who went through any kind of abuse. The most helpful tool I found is *The Courage to Heal*,[7] a book which is subtitled 'A guide for women survivors of child sexual abuse' but which works as well for any kind of emotional or physical abuse and for men as well as women. If you feel that you have been abused, or if you know this to be so, then this book can help you.

A good counsellor or psychotherapist can also help, but you should ensure that this is someone who really under-stands and who can help you to access the memories and deal with the pain as well as building up trust and intimacy. Support, persistence and compassion for yourself and what you went through are vital during this process. As the victims of sexual abuse have usually been alone with their secret for too long, a self-help group can be fertile ground for learning to share feelings once again and will bring a sense of empathy and understanding to aid the healing pro-cess. It is possible to heal and your life will be enriched by so doing.

THE NEW SEXUALITY

The menopause heralds a new era of sexual freedom, a release from the need for contraception, and the opportunity to explore many more facets of our sexuality. Many women report an upsurge of new energy as the menopause draws to its close and this can be a time of great creative activity and self-expression on all levels. Menopausal women appear to have everything to look forward to and limitless oppor-tunity to celebrate the joy of life through their sexuality.

EXERCISE

Create your own sexual ritual and act this out either with your partner or through active imagination, dance, and such like. Don't be afraid to take a risk. You might like to experiment with being photographed or filmed in order to portray your sexuality. You may decide to change your image totally and present a new face to the world.

This is your opportunity to use all the creative energy you have generated and to incorporate all the facets of your sexuality that you have discovered. Be adventurous and express your needs fully to your partner (or to yourself). You and your relationship can only benefit from an expression of who you are.

6. ✦ *The Mythic Dimension*

When a woman senses that there is a mythic dimension to something she is undertaking, that knowledge touches and inspires deep creative centers in her.[1]

Jean Shinoda Bolen

THE ETERNAL FEMININE

For many years now, through my astrological studies, I have been aware of how myth reflects and elucidates archetypal human experience. An archetype is a universal symbol, an inherited mental image to which humankind responds, and which is often acted upon as an unconscious reaction to human experience. The eternally youthful *puer* or *puella* (Latin, *boy, girl*) is, for instance, one response to ageing. The puella simply refused to grow up and acts in an insouciant, irresponsible way. She is eternally 'Daddy's little girl'. The aged Crone is another archetype, and one that often strikes fear into the hearts of men (and many women) because she has, in their eyes, tremendous power and cannot be confined.

Myth is an inner truth, also from the collective level of experience, which is presented through images and symbols that resonate within our psyche. It cannot be apprehended by the rational mind, belonging to the feminine realm of intuition and knowing. It is something we inherit from our ancestors and it touches a cord in the genetic, racial memory. The themes it personifies are eternal, relevant to every generation, evoking feelings and images from the depths of our psyche. Using myth enables our imagination to present us with our own particular truth.

In psychological astrology the planets, and the mythological figures attached to them, represent energies and drives within us. I feel that the goddesses, and their mythological context, have much to tell us about feminine psychology. Each goddess can be seen as an archetype, representing certain of our inner drives or qualities, which may be consciously or unconsciously expressed in our life. As such, the goddesses can be extremely useful in developing neglected or hidden potential, or certain personality traits such as assertion, confidence, etc. which would be useful to us. I have for some time been using active imagination to contact the specific energies which the goddesses signify. Active imagination is the art of using symbols and images to talk to, and activate, the unconscious part of our mind within which this archetypal energy is held. It is a simple technique which requires nothing other than a willingness to let go and see what emerges from your own psyche, and yet it can set in motion constructive change and new experiences.

My interest in the link between myth and the menopause was therefore stimulated when my partner, Robert Jacobs, mentioned that, in a homoeopathic lecture given some years earlier, Dr June Burger had stated that each of the 'Seven Ages of Woman' had its own goddess. She designated Hera as the goddess who watches over the menopause. In her view, Hera was the professional woman who has brought up her family and become a woman in her own right – a stage that few women reached before they were forty five. If the woman knew where she was going, she had no menopausal symptoms.

I was more familiar with the notion of Hera as wife, 'the power behind the throne' type of woman, and I commented that I had always found Hera a rather boring figure, although I could, somewhat unwillingly, identify with the rage and jealousy of her dark side when I later researched her. I much preferred Demeter who, according to Dr Burger, watched over the final age of woman and who was wise and loving, all the family coming back to her for her wisdom. She is, however, also an archetype of the grieving mother whose children have left home and whose life becomes barren and, therefore, is very suitable to watch over the menopause.

ENCOUNTERING THE GODDESSES

At this stage two books[2] synchronistically arrived in my possession. Both were about the goddesses within women and how attunement to a particular goddess archetype shapes women's behaviour: each goddess representing a different quality such as wisdom, nurturing, assertion, vulnerability, self-sufficiency, dependency, destruction, creativity, and so on. Both books also suggested that 'lack' of a certain goddess may indicate an area to be worked on or integrated. I was not, therefore, surprised to find that, when I added up my score on the 'Goddess Wheel' in *The Goddess Within*, −1 appeared under Hera.

The authors, Jennifer and Roger Woolger, see the six Greek goddesses who appear in their book as aspects of 'The Great Mother' and Hera was the 'Power' aspect. She is seen as 'empress, ruler, wife, worldly power, tradition, marriage, partnership, morality, matriarch', areas of life which which I felt little connection and yet I knew that exploring, and owning, my power was a major theme at this stage in my life. Clearly, I needed to make contact with Hera.

Predictably perhaps, my highest score was Persephone, the 'Underworld' aspect of the goddess, who rules 'occult, medium, clairvoyance, visions, dreams, death and trans-formation, inner guide, healing, psychic power': all areas of life with which I felt very much at home and which I had been living out for the past seventeen years. My second highest score surprised me a little at first. Artemis is the 'Nature' aspect of the goddess, associated with 'Amazon, shamaness, blood mysteries, adventures, huntress, lover of wilderness, lady of the beasts'; but my connection to her became clearer whilst writing this book and Nor Hall's description of her[3] as the midwife who teaches others how to survive contact with the energies of the unconscious fitted my work well. My changing role in life was clear from my second lowest score. According to the Woolgers, Demeter is the 'Mother' aspect of the goddess, associated with 'body as vessel, lady of plants, menstruation, child-bearing, earth mother, generation, nurturance, daughter': the areas which were passing out of my personal life.

The influence of the goddesses interweave and alternate throughout life. The midlife, or post-hysterectomy, stage especially is one where the repressed or unmanifested energies represented by the goddesses will suddenly emerge, causing 'out of character' behaviour as a new archetype struggles to be expressed – and usually horrifying the family who put it all down to 'her age, you know'. This is the time when the previously homeloving and passive wife (Demeter, Hestia or Hera) may suddenly start going to classes or workshops to develop her neglected intellect (Athena) or psychic powers (Persephone or the other face of Hestia). Hecate may emerge, urging her into therapy to collect together the scattered parts of herself: Artemis rising will enable her to holiday alone, or get a divorce, or perhaps to enter a lesbian relationship for the first time. Aphrodite may come to the fore, resulting perhaps in an affair or a surge of artistic energy; or Demeter may emerge in a career woman causing her to fall into the deep depression of the 'empty nest' syndrome.

However, if these goddesses can be seen as positive opportunities to explore new possibilities and ways of interacting with the world, the midlife stage of life offers the excitement of exploring the unrecognized parts of ourselves and rounding out our experience. Rather than selecting 'acceptable' parts to present to ourselves and others, thereby fragmenting and cutting ourselves off from our fundamental nature, if we can recognize that 'all this is me', we can return to a state of integration and wholeness which encompasses the totality of our female nature.

Whilst different goddess personas may be unconsciously activated by changes, it is possible to invoke or consciously to adopt others, as in the exercises below. You may like to identify women in your life who epitomize 'missing' qualities and study how they use the energy. Mothers, mothers-in-law and grandmothers, aunts, friends and sisters are all fruitful sources of the goddesses, as are 'superiors' on the career ladder or women who have achieved something you are striving for – who can be useful role models or mentors as you struggle to express the new energy. Mentors are particularly useful to have at times of change. They are people – in the case of the menopause, women who have successfully made the transition into the Wise Woman – who can oversee and guide your progress and who are able to offer helpful advice from time to time.

Another way to identify a 'missing' goddess is to think of someone you particularly dislike. Is she bossy, matriarchal, dominant and controlling, possessive, ambitious for her husband or son? Then she is probably portraying the destructive side of the Hera archetype to you, and may well be reflecting back the unacknowledged, shadow, side of yourself as she does for me. I am always uneasily aware, however, that these qualities lurk just below the surface. Therefore I am endeavouring to integrate these qualities and claim the constructive and creative power of which they are the shadow. I know that once I can own this power I will have finally moved into the Wise Woman side of my nature.

EXERCISE
Identifying the goddesses in your life

1. Appendix II contains profiles of some of the goddesses who are most relevant to the midlife transition. Identify which of the goddesses are prominent and which are missing in your life now. If necessary, refer back to the life statement you made in Chapter 4. (You may also like to refer to the 'Goddess Wheel' in *The Goddess Within*.[2]) Look back over your life and identify when changes in the goddess energies took place. Is there a goddess who would give you something you feel you lack now? Is one struggling to emerge? If so, how can you help her?
2. Study someone you admire, envy or wish to emulate. Which goddesses are active in her life? How does she use them? How do her qualities relate to your own? How can you integrate these energies positively into yourself?
3. Study someone you dislike or feel uncomfortable with. What does she tell you about the shadow side of yourself? How can you make this energy more conscious, and therefore more constructive, within yourself?

AN ANCIENT ENERGY

The goddesses are not limited to the Greek system, which, in any case incorporated (and 'sanitized') much older, and darker goddesses such as Hecate and Artemis. Even Hera is believed to be an earlier matriarchal goddess who was incorporated into the patriarchal Greek world by expedient marriage to Zeus. The older goddesses such as Kali, Ishtar and Lilith, whose origins are much further east, all have the characteristic of incorporating both dark and light, creation and destruction, preservation and dissolution, action and passivity, within themselves. They epitomize the birth-death-rebirth cycle of the ancient mysteries and of human experience, indicating humanity's need to attune to the natural rhythms of creation.

As Edward Whitmont explains: 'In the older goddess representations . . . we still find the complementary aspects of engendering life, love and joy, as well as revelling in suffering, destruction and death. This duality of function emotionally encompasses the actual fullness of existence, the *no* phase which we have repressed . . .'[4] The 'no phase' is the right to say 'no, that is enough'. It is detachment and rejection, it is letting go in order that something new may flourish. It is the outer world reflecting the need to make way for inner change and regeneration. It is the awe and fear ancient man felt for nature and he, therefore, both respected and worshipped her in all her manifestations. It is the process of creativity at work.

It is this power to say 'No' that most terrified man (and caused the suppression of the goddess) because it links into the primal need for mothering and nurturing. There is an inextricable bond between women and nurturing. In a man's eyes, every woman is Mother, 'the Great No-Sayer' of childhood, the fount of existence and the threat of annihilation. If women say 'No' they become the Devouring Mother of childhood nightmare, that side of the goddess that men have feared since time began because those who can give life can also take it away.

However, the 'duality of function' is something that humanity desperately needs to regain at this stage in its evolution, something which womankind in particular can restore to its rightful place in human consciousness. In *The Book of Lilith*,[5] Barbara Black Koltuv sees Lilith as 'that part of the Great Goddess that has been rejected and cast out'. She identifies various qualities such as lunar consciousness and its connection to the cycles of life; instinctual, earthy sexuality; prophetic inner knowledge; and finally the primal creativity of the Goddess, all of which must be reclaimed by women in order to make themselves whole and redeem themselves from being 'spiritual outcasts' and thereby return balance and equilibrium to the earth.

It is these 'dark' goddesses with their strong links to the Moon who have the greatest relevance to women's 'wise blood' and what Peter Redgrove calls 'womb knowledge'[6] an ancient knowing that is older than time. As he points out, the Hebrew Talmud sees a child in the womb as 'the Ancient of Days', knowing everything. At its birth, however, an angel wipes away the memory of that knowledge with its wings. In the recent historical past, menstrual blood has been feared by man and bound with taboos. As late as the sixteenth century, European witches were believed to attain their magical powers from the retention of their wise 'Moon blood'[7] and one of the 'reasons' for burning Joan of Arc was that she did not menstruate.

In earlier matriarchal times, however, menstruation was honoured and sanctified as 'wise blood', a gift from the goddess. This wise blood solidified into life itself. Matriarchy was crucial to the survival of the tribe because uterine blood, the 'Moon flower' of which the 'Moon seed' was a child, contained the soul essence of future generations. Indeed, the 'life' that arose out of the waters at creation can be seen as an allegory for the womb experience. In all the early creation myths the formless flux, or chaos, of creation corresponds to the uterine environment. Its watery depths are dark and rhythmic, reflecting the dimly remembered life in the uterus.

It is, of course, obvious to anyone who has carried a child that the foetus is aware of, and reacts to, its environment from a very early age and many of the mythological components may arise from this primal experience. The experience of carrying a child, naturally, is one which women share but from which men are excluded. However, everyone shares the experience of mother as all-powerful, filling the world: indeed, being the world for the first nine months. Her emotional highs and lows, with the attendant chemical changes in the body, are experienced by the foetus as all-consuming, a totality of overwhelming sensation. And, as psychologists have found, the drama and trauma of birth imprints itself indelibly on the consciousness. Small wonder, then, that the creation stories should contain a mythic element founded in the womb and its visible mystery, menstrual blood; and that the immanent Mother Goddess should be an integral part of her creation, rather than separate as is the patriarchal God-the-father.

In the earliest Mesopotamian creation stories, Adam (or 'first man') is created by the Goddess out of moon blood and clay. The Hindus believed that the Great Mother Goddess gave birth to the cosmos out of the primal flux (her menstrual blood). The South American Indians thought mankind was made of 'moon blood', and the Koran states that Allah 'made man out of flowing blood' (a clot formed, and became man). This link between blood and life continued into patriarchal times, although by then the part the father played was understood. The writer of the *Wisdom of Solomon* (part of the biblical Apocrypha) says 'In my mother's womb I was wrought into flesh during a ten month space [lunar months] compacted in blood, from the seed of her husband and the pleasure that is joined with sleep' (7:2). According to Deuteronomy, 'The blood is the life' (12:23), notwithstanding that, by the time Deuteronomy was written it is shed by man through sacrifice rather than being an inherent sacred function of woman.

In many of the ancient wisdom sources it is this 'moon blood' or menstruation which is linked both to the life essence of creation *and* to spiritual illumination. Kali invites the gods to bathe in the bloody flow of her womb and to drink of it, and gods drink of the 'waters of life' and are blessed. The god Thor reached the land of enlightenment by bathing in a river of menstrual blood, and Odin gained his supremacy by drinking from the cauldron of wise blood belonging to Mother Earth. The Egyptian pharaohs sought divinity through drinking the 'blood of Isis'. The Celtic gods obtained their divine nature from the 'red mead' of the faery queen, and the Greeks used what was euphemistically called 'Hera's supernatural red wine' in their sacred mystery rites of rebirth (whenever wine or the waters of life are mentioned in myth, it is almost certain to be referring to menstrual blood). The Australian aborigines linked rebirth to menstrual blood.[8]

In ancient China, tantra taught that men could become immortal by absorbing menstrual blood from 'woman's mysterious gateway' and the Kaula Tantra informs us that:

> The Tantric Adept should view a menstruating woman with reverence and awe. She is the living embodiment of Kali, the power of transcendence; her menstrual blood is the flowery essence of all mankind, the very blood of life. Possessed of supernormal qualities, it is a potent rejuvenating and transforming force, purifying all poisons through its alchemical fire. By performing sexual rites with a menstruating woman, the Adept can more quickly advance along the Path of Liberation.[9]

Red ochre is used in sacred ceremonies throughout the world in the belief that it is the goddess's sacred blood and the supervision of these rites is usually in the hands of the old women, those who are retaining their 'wise blood'. In many ancient cultures a special place was set aside for menstruating women as they were believed to be more psychically open at this time and susceptible to influences from the 'other world'. Traditionally such places were supervised by the post-menstrual Wise Women who taught them crafts, arts, ritual songs and spiritual traditions. 'In particular this was a time to learn the legends of the tribe, the lineage of the family, and to become acquainted with the powers of transcendence.'[10]

In his far-ranging book *The Black Goddess*, which explores these ideas, Peter Redgrove sees menstruation as a sacred sacrifice of great power and says, 'It is as though in humans the womb were re-made to bleed in order to open that crack between the worlds, *as though menstruation were there to activate the blood-threshold, to render it familiar and kind, to overcome the birth trauma and to give resurrection by womb-knowledge* . . . This may be the pattern intended from the beginning, when black Wisdom offered the red menstrual fruit of the Tree to the first black Adam.'[11]

It is the women who have retained this wise blood, those who have crossed through the initiation of menopause, who can lead the return of this hidden knowledge so intimately bound up with woman's menstrual cycle. This is how it used to be. Those who had moved beyond shedding the sacred blood became the priestesses, seers, healers and mid-wives leading the tribe to spiritual illumination. They were Wise Women.

Attunement to the ancient goddesses, and to the natural rhythms with which they resonate, takes one into the dark recesses of the psyche and of the human unconscious, to a place where integration and healing are possible. The god-desses experienced the basic archetypal experiences of woman: birth and death, loss and renunciation, abuse and humiliation, passion and jealousy, creation and illumination. They are familiar with the territory, and so are available to act as a guide to a woman undergoing these same passages. The waning-moon goddess Hecate, for instance, lived in a cave at the entrance to the underworld. Goddess of the crossroads, she has a torch to light the darkness and brings together lost parts of the self. This is one of the major reasons for studying the goddesses; to reunite parts of your-self and to re-assimilate the ancient wisdom they represent.

With the synchronicity I was beginning to expect when dealing with the goddesses, as soon as I had finished draft-ing this chapter a friend who had just been through a traumatic divorce came to stay. She shared with me her own experiences of attuning to a goddess and her verbatim report shows just how powerful the experience can be:

> I wanted to do it because first of all *The Goddess Within* gave me Aphrodite and, although she is the one that people pick for me, I didn't feel 100 per cent in touch with her. The more I read about her, the more I felt she was a lot to do with my outer appearance and nothing to do with my inner being. I wasn't connecting at a deep level. Also I wanted to stir up my creativity and it seemed to be the most suitable goddess for that because I wanted to expand not just my writing but to colour, painting – to add a width to my creativity which I felt was lacking.
>
> The desire to contact her got stronger and stronger. It was an intuitive thing, so what I did was to make my own ritual. I got a statuette of her which my brothers had given me which is a reproduction of a statue of her dancing, with skirts flying, and she's holding a fruit, so I thought I'd use that. I got pink candles, because of the colour. Then I picked some roses, her flowers, and I decided to do it in my bedroom as the most

suitable room. I got some really beautiful music and I got everything ready beforehand, very consciously with great intent. I had a bath and burnt incense to make a sweet smell. I sat and read for about an hour, all the different stories about her and her aspects.

I kept looking at the statue and I discovered if I put the candle in a certain position the shadow of her danced on the wall. So, from the dancing shadow, I filled her out until she was real. The shadow moving with the candle flame and her skirt, which was wrapped round her hips, flying out was so real, it was beautiful. You could see her arms leading forward and everything, and I made her real from that. I gradually felt her dance, and it was the dance I wanted. I wanted that insouciance, that humorous, joyful stuff from her.

I must say to begin with I felt a bit like a 'nana sitting all by myself in my bedroom. But I said: 'Hail Aphrodite', I really spoke to her like I imagined you would speak to her: 'Aphrodite, goddess of love, goddess of art, goddess of dance' and I went on like that. I then shut my eyes because I had got the image of her by then in my inner vision. I relaxed my body and lay down on the bed, and started to feel her inside me, and feel that golden light round her and her fruit and flowers, and all those things. It got beyond petitioning an archetype, it became more that she was there dancing in my heart centre, it was like her little figure was small at first and then getting bigger and bigger filling me and at the same time separate. It was extraordinary, absolutely extraordinary. It was the way she grew out of my centre and filled me up. My whole body felt tingly, it was a very physical thing, it was inside my flesh and blood. I am a person who can easily go 'floaty-floaty', so I was very impressed that this was in my body. I was talking to her and saying, 'Please help me dance through these times which are putting shackles on my limbs and weighting me down.' Her joy and her sailing on the sea foam and all those things, I wanted those sensations quite badly.

Anyway, I went on for a good hour and it grew very late and I decided it had been so powerful I must shut off, so I saw myself in Greece walking back up a beach from the edge of the sea and going through an archway and climbing back up to ordinary land away from the sea. Then I visualized a huge big old door which I opened and stood outside, and bid her farewell and asked her that she should stay with me and protect me but I was saying farewell for the time being. And then I closed the door very firmly because I wasn't really sure what I might have stirred up, and went to sleep. I slept very deeply for a long time, which I hadn't been doing, and the next day I felt unbelievable. I kept feeling the feeling of it while I was doing very ordinary things, and I had a tremendous burst of energy and I got very determined to get the house looking as beautiful as I could and in my mind I was thinking I was partly doing that for her and partly getting everything ready for something which I felt was coming to do with her. So I was clearing the decks, and getting rid of anything dark or old or untidy or falling to bits, because it wasn't appropriate any more to have those things around.

This is going to sound completely mad but I felt like I was in love and there isn't anyone, but I felt that wonderful feeling when you are really in love and it was very sensual but it wasn't sexual specifically. It was this fabulous feeling and I felt like that for several days. I felt fantastic and I got an idea for a play that I want to write, out of the blue. I kept getting flowers brought me, which I thought was significant, and a couple of really nice things happened and I felt very protected.

And the other powerful thing is that because I used that little statuette in that way, and of course it's still by my bed where it's always been, now when I look at it it is filled with something far more than merely a pretty object, it's filled with something powerful and it kicks me back off again. The feeling still hasn't gone away and I'm beginning to understand the power of objects and paintings. She is the nearest to what I feel is my essence, she is like a sister to the part of me that I can contact easily. I need the balance.

This same friend had Kali as her guide during psychotherapy, indicating the ubiquitous and universal nature of the great goddesses, which crosses cultural boundaries in response to individual feminine need.

Each culture has its own goddesses and I have mentioned the ones with which I have some familiarity. I am aware, however, that other cultures have their own particular myths and goddesses with whom I am, as yet, out of touch. Each individual woman will have a goddess with whom she will particularly identify and with whom she can resonate, even though this may be at the level below consciousness. Many women find that images of the goddess spontaneously emerge in their dreams during the time of transition. Images of the goddess include maidens, old crones, mirrors, cauldrons, spindles, looms, bows, sickles, moons, grain, pomegranates, caverns, wells, bees, serpents, spiders, cows, eggs, does, and many more, including of course the lioness or cat.

My own particular resonance is the Egyptian lion-goddess, Sekhmet. I first encountered her in the British Museum, but her energy vibrated within me when I stepped into an evocative room at the Louvre and looked down a long row of enigmatic leonine smiles. A deeper attunement developed in Egypt, particularly in her special temple at Karnak, the Mut (or Birth/Initiation) Temple, from which these statues had been removed. The temple was closed to tourists and therefore held a sense of immense peace and ancient tranquillity. Her greatest impact came, however, in an even more appropriate setting. The 'guardians' at Karnak take great delight in showing adventurous tourists one of the hidden treasures of the main temple. Tucked away in sand dunes there is a small, unruined temple, a place of great power. Secluded behind closed doors is a towering statue of Sekhmet, lit only by a single shaft of light from a hole in the ceiling. An awesome sight indeed. The guardian introduced us to the 'Blessing of Sekhmet' which he said was an ancient ritual, but even if it was something concocted for the tourists it was certainly effective!

I instinctively feel that Sekhmet has great relevance for menopausal women. The daughter of Ra, the sun god, she was unleashed in all her destructive awesomeness when his subjects displeased him, and shed gallons of blood. Ra changed his mind and sent a baboon-god to bring her back. Drugged and tricked into submission, she was told humorous stories to keep her quiet. Eventually she became a goddess of healing, birth and initiation. Married to Ptah, the builder-creator god who was known as the Architect of the Universe, Sekhmet epitomizes the cycle of destruction of the old in order to make way for the new: the birth-death-rebirth cycle. She and Ptah are both a duality and a unity. Her plight reminds me of woman: sent to this earth with her sacred blood, woman has nevertheless been restrained and pacified and must find a way to move into the role of transformer and healer, if she is once again to fulfil her purpose in life and birth her own sacred nature.

In his book *The Goddess Sekhmet*[12] Robert Masters describes being entranced in front of a statue of the goddess. In a powerful experience, Sekhmet became a living reality for him. As he warns in the introduction to the book, the experience can be both numinous and full of terror, as befitted a goddess who is 'Lady of Transformation' and 'of the Bloodbath'. The exercise below has been adapted from Robert Masters' work, and should be approached with caution. You may find it preferable to begin on one of the 'lighter' goddesses, although even Aphrodite, the goddess of love, had her dark side. The exercise introduces the immense creative power of these archetypal images, and helps you to incorporate your own dark side into consciousness.

In my own experience, Sekhmet has shown me her healing side. During my first visualization, when I was using Robert Masters' technique, I was filled with a powerful radiant energy and was aware of the goddess smiling down at me and then lifting me up to her level. Later, in psychosynthesis therapy, which uses visualization, Sekhmet came as my inner guide and took me to an Egyptian tomb – appropriately that of Queen Hatshepsut, one of the first militant feminists, who stole the power from her young brother/husband and became an extremely effective ruler in her own right. In her temple, Hatshepsut is portrayed in the guise of Hathor, an 'earth mother' goddess whose dark side incorporates the goddess Sekhmet but who is also a goddess of beauty, love, music and the sacred marriage. By being so portrayed, Hatshepsut was taking on the qualities of this goddess.

When Sekhmet took me to Hatshepsut's tomb in the visualization, we went in through the 'back door', a tomb belonging to her architect (a familiar spot I had visited when in Egypt). In actuality this tomb has a long tunnel under the mountain which separates Hatshepsut's temple from the Valley of the Queens – something I had tried not to think about as I crouched on the second level 150 feet below the entrance and several hundred feet below the summit of the mountain. It was horribly reminiscent of the birth canal and a place of overwhelming power. In Egypt, architects were partakers in the sacred mysteries and it is likely that the connection between the two tombs has an esoteric significance. Only two levels of steps in the tomb have been excavated so, in the imaging, I had an exhilarating slide down the long ramp, and arrived in an undignified heap on top of the goddess, who was unperturbed and told me I had finally learned to let go! We came out into an empty burial chamber, which was gradually furnished and painted with huge images of the gods and goddesses as the therapy progressed.

Over the weeks and months of this work, I became aware of an attunement to a deep source of creative energy within myself, which was mirrored in the 'tomb' and which ultimately resulted in this book. Appropriately, each time we emerged through the 'front door' in the Valley of the Queens, I felt a sense of rebirth. I had ventured into the underworld and survived. In another, actual, visit to Egypt I was puffing my way up a very steep ladder from the

Fig. 10   Hatshepsut portrayed in the guise of the benevolent goddess Hathor

depths of a pharaoh's tomb and grumbled to Robert Jacobs that 'they didn't have old grannies in mind when they built these places'. Rob's response was to point out that 'old grannies were not meant to come out again!'. 'Well, this one has', I retorted with glee and a new surge of energy as I reconnected to my imaging.

ATTUNING TO THE GODDESSES

Before commencing this exercise, study the goddesses and select the one that resonates with you. Read as many different versions of her myth as possible, study it until you instinctively understand. If possible, visit a statue of the goddess (most big museums have at least one and many of them were magically impregnated with the essence of the goddess as part of the temple rituals).

Next, find some pictures of the goddess (the *Larousse Encyclopaedia of Mythology* is a useful source). Choose the picture which you feel most captures the qualities of the goddess and sketch, draw, paint or model this for yourself. It does not need to be a work of art, as my own sketch

Fig. 11   Sekhmet

shows; the aim is to attune to the energy and, eventually, to memorize the statue. If possible, frame your sketch and hang it in a place where you will see it often.

Meeting the goddess

Choosing a quiet time and place where you will not be disturbed, and using the picture or the statue you have chosen, spend a few moments breathing gently and focusing your thoughts on the goddess.

When you are completely relaxed, ask that the goddess will manifest for you. Then, beginning with the head, focus your attention on the statue of the goddess until it begins to live. Pay special attention to the eyes, looking deep into these and connecting to the being who lives behind them. Slowly work down the statue until you have a living picture in your mind.

At this point close your eyes and concentrate on the inner image, inviting her to manifest her energy within you. Look at life through her eyes. She may take you back to relive her myth, she may take you into an inner experience. Do not be afraid; allow the goddess to reveal to you what you need to know.

When the experience is over, thank her for coming and ask her to be available to you in the future. Slowly open your eyes and take time to adjust to being back in the outer world. Then write your experiences up in your journal, using the present tense to reinforce the experience.

This visualization should be repeated daily until the goddess is experienced as a living presence. The exercise can then be repeated to contact an energy which is 'missing' or one of which you are fearful or which you would like to utilize in your life.

THE SACRED MARRIAGE

Having re-membered all the parts of your feminine psyche through attunement to the goddesses, it is now time to reintegrate the masculine energies which also form part of your self. Every woman is a complex mix of male and female: consciously or unconsciously, these energies are expressed in our daily life and, in order to be whole, we need to be able to access, integrate and, above all, use all our qualities as appropriate.

Many of the old religions featured the sacred marriage, a uniting of the male and female energies represented by the god and goddess, and this was an important aspect of many initiation ceremonies. Although the ritual would vary, often incorporating the god and goddess through surrogates such as a priest and priestess and frequently including the whole congregation in the 'orgy' that followed, the essence of the ritual remained the same: a linking of the energies of the earth mother with the sky god, the consequent fertilization and renewal of the earth, and, simultaneously, a uniting of masculine and feminine within the celebrants and an attunement to the cosmic energies behind creation.

This is the sacred marriage of the alchemists. The inner marriage can be an important part of woman's spiritual development as it enables her to reclaim the power normally projected onto a convenient male and gives her access to the 'masculine' qualities of action and initiation. The 'marriage within' is to her own instinctual and sacred nature, the 'god within'; it reveals the true nature of love rather than the sexual desire or conditional approval which so often passes for love. Such an inner marriage cannot be forced. It arises spontaneously in dreams – often through sexual intercourse with a male figure or by phallic symbols and 'mirror images' (which should be recorded in your journal or painted to make them live) – but it can be invoked by the use of active imagination.

Although it is possible to tape the exercise, leaving plenty of time to follow the instructions, it is better to memorize it as this enables you to follow your own inner timing – along with any images which may arise spontaneously as you progress.

EXERCISE
Making the inner marriage

Choosing a quiet time when you will be undisturbed, sit or lie with your eyes closed. Gently breathe out any tension you may be feeling and breathe in a sense of peace and relaxation. When you are fully relaxed, centre your attention between your eye-brows.

Picture yourself walking up a paved way towards a temple. Feel your feet on the sunwarmed stones. On either side is a row of cypress trees; above you is a clear blue sky. As you enter the temple, you will see that, on your left, there is a quiet, airy room with a pool where a female attendant waits to bathe and dress you.

When she has prepared and perfumed you, she will gesture to the right side of the temple. Here a male figure awaits you. He will conduct you through the columned arcades of the temple to the chamber where you will spend the night. Here your bride-groom is waiting. Leave your inhibitions at the door as you enter and move towards the sacred marriage bed. The lovemaking will be wild and abandoned, tender and gentle, connecting to the primal energies and touching a wellspring of creativity within you (you may even find that you birth a sacred child as a result of this night). Your bridegroom will give you his qualities, enabling you to find them within yourself, to merge and integrate into wholeness.

When you are ready to leave, thank him and say goodbye, retaining his qualities within yourself. Ask him to be with you when needed. The attendant will then conduct you back through the temple to the gateway. As you walk down the paved way, begin to return your awareness to the room.

When you have completed the visualization, open your eyes and quietly reflect for a few moments and then record your experience in your journal, or paint a symbolic picture which captures the essence to remind you.

You may like to extend this exploration of the masculine energies to a study of the mythic consort of the goddess who survived into historical times as 'The Green Man'. Alan Richardson's book *Earth God Rising*[13] is extremely useful in this respect. Reading about this fascinating figure, sketching him or finding his image in old churches will help you to attune to the balancing energy within nature, so that you can find the point of equilibrium within yourself.

Now that you have attuned to these archetypal forces and the enormous power they possess, you will find that you experience a tremendous surge of creative energy which can be put to work for the final stage of growth: the movement into the Wise Woman archetype, a period of expansion following the psychological integration of the different parts of your self. This is the moment when everything becomes possible, when the infinite possibilities open to the 'woman of a certain age' can attain fullness.

7. ❖ The Wise Woman

The archetypal role of the new femininity is to stand as priestess to the fullness of life.[1]

Edward Whitmont

THE CULTURAL BACKGROUND

Before this century, the life expectancy of women was low and comparatively few women reached the menopause. It seems strange, therefore, to find little trace of anything to mark this significant milestone. However, anthropologist Judith K. Brown, in a wide-ranging cross-cultural study of middle-aged women,[2] found that it was typical for menopause not to be marked by a rite but that, nevertheless, it was an important transition as it signified a new liberty. In a much earlier study, Margaret Mead had looked at the status of women in over a hundred cultures and found one constant: in each, the role of women was reversed at menopause.

In most 'primitive', patriarchal societies, this change in status is linked to the lifting of taboos that surround menstruation and which prescribe a woman's role and status in that society. Judith Brown found that, in most of the non-industrial societies in her study, this is one of three significant changes which take place; the others being that women are expected to assume responsibility for, and authority over, younger kin and that they are then eligible for special roles within the community such as midwives, healers, givers of initiation, holy women, matchmakers and 'guardians of the sacred hearth'.

Maori women, for instance, become the formal mourners at funeral rites, and instruct the younger women in traditional arts and crafts, as well as taking part in ritual ceremonies. In Bali, not only can the post-menopausal women take part in ceremonies with the virgins, but they can also use obscene language without censure. In certain parts of India, women can discard the veil after the meno-pause, and in many other societies the travel restrictions are lifted so women become traders and marriage brokers, or administer the kin system and the social life of the extended family group, all of which give post-menopausal women considerable power in the community.

This greatly enhanced status reverses the powerless, some-what passive role that menstruating, and therefore child-rearing, women usually have in the society and opens the way for the women's self-development. As Paula Weideger points out in her historical survey of menstruation and menopause: 'When the taboo lifts at menopause, a woman is given freedom to become a self-defined person'.[3] And anthropologist Richard Lee describes post-menopausal women as the 'movers and shakers' of Kung society.[4] The older Kung women have a great deal of sexual freedom, often taking much younger lovers, making lewd jokes and instigating a great deal of sexual horseplay such as grabbing men's genitals in public.

The Kung, a hunter-gatherer tribe from southern Africa, traditionally breastfeed their children for several years and the women rarely experience the menopause as a physio-logical event, merely finding that, around the age of forty when they stop breastfeeding the last child, menstruation does not recommence. The link between breastfeeding and the hormones produced during lactation may well be one reason why women in these traditional societies do not usually experience any symptoms at menopause, other than cessation of bleeding. Research does vary on whether or not such women experience menopausal symptoms so one cannot draw too dogmatic a conclusion here. However, they do have a socially defined, and valued, role to move into.

In almost all the societies studied, post-menopausal women retained, or even expanded upon, their sexual role. The exception was women from southern Asia where tra-dition demanded that older men, and therefore women by default, cease from intercourse in order to retain their 'essence' (strength) and to develop their spiritual nature. In some southern Asian communities, sex with an older woman was considered positively dangerous and life-threatening, even to the extent of being fatal. Parents were expected to refrain from intercourse once their eldest son married and a woman who became pregnant after this event was seen as a scandal, something to be ashamed of.

Finding time for the older couple to be alone together was difficult. As the researcher pointed out, in most families the grandparents were living with their married children and the younger couple would send their children to sleep with the grandparents in order to retain privacy for themselves. The older men were, in any case, encouraged to leave their families and go off on a spiritual search. This often left the older women in a position of matriarchal power, but as a sexless being. After menopause the southern Asian woman was able to achieve the 'ideal', a pure, sexless and totally benevolent mother image.[5] She was, as with all the other mature women in the study, a figure of power.

Analyzing the cross-cultural study, David Gutmann, a developmental psychologist, feels that this universal advance in the position of women across such varied social settings, and the accompanying rise to power, is a phenomenon beyond culture. It is his argument that this is a natural progression and development for woman, an activation of her latent powers, and that when this developmental right is overlooked, the 'denigrating view' of the post-menopausal woman as a helpless victim takes over, to the detriment of the community. This inherent progression has been arrested in the industrialized nations of the West, who have lost their contact with the natural rhythm of the entire feminine cycle. Now it is time to reclaim that latent power so that women can blossom into the fullness of their prime.

'AN INCHOATE LONGING'

I have found that many women in their mid-forties have a yearning which they find hard to articulate, a feeling that 'there must be more than this'. One of my clients described it as an 'inchoate longing, having neither form nor consciousness, for something *other*'. The following letter is typical of those I receive asking for astrological readings at this time:

> For the past couple of years I have been experiencing a sense of futility about my life. Indeed, I have never achieved very much despite an enormous number of 'talents'. In particular I give so little, to others or even to the planet in general. I deplore the waste but don't know how to change.

Those who have reached their fifties put it even more strongly.

Women are, I believe, reaching out to the spiritual dimension of life which is, for most of us, so lacking today. As *The Spiral Path* points out, 'Women's experiences of nothingness and worthlessness often precede an awakening to new sources of power and spirit'.[6] In the same book, David Fish identifies three 'spurs' to spiritual growth. These are a deep dissatisfaction with life as it is currently experienced; pain, which tells us something is wrong and must be looked at; and a vision of something higher. The experience of a workshop participant makes this clear:

> I, as a married woman, fought for my space in my marriage. Suffocating in order to find the 'lost soul' within me.
>
> My husband would use intimidation and oppressed me in a systematic way to hold his power over me, the proverbial Doormat. This holding power, which was perhaps labelled as love originally in the marriage, manifested itself as an attack on my menopausal age group, a very sensitive area. Verbal abuse such as: 'You're sick', 'Go and see your doctor', 'You're round the twist', etc. All these comments, so cruel, were usually in response to me asking – pleading – for more love, sexual attention, and a quality awareness in the marriage. Such comments, when made, succeeded in promptly knocking me off my feminine pedestal, only once more to recoil into my private sad world of mid-life confusion.
>
> I was trapped in the role play of redundant mother and perpetual housekeeper, knowing that the tenderness that was once there is no longer, and possibly never will return. But I hung on in there, in hope, 'knowing' that the marriage was dead, had been for years.
>
> The fear (and I do believe that this is the feeling related to all moves on most levels, pleasant and unpleasant), the unknown, the insecurity of moving out of a dead marriage is traumatic, especially if this involves leaving teenage children as

in my case. A test indeed that has proved very valid before the long leap takes place. One feels a 'death' inside one's soul.

'Deathness' instigates rebirth and this is the threshold realization of not looking back, but proceeding forward into the unknown, as in fact death would appear. Then, and only then can a woman find her true self as I have done, meeting her own needs first and recognizing the others will do the same thing in response. A change of energy is the most energizing stimulus to any blocked situation. My two teenage daughters have changed and gained an emotional responsibility of their own, making what I am sure will be a wonderful foundation for their future development, spiritually and practically in their daily lives. My invisible thread of 'umbilical love' will always be for me, and I hope for them, permanently connected. The 'knowing' of love is a precious gift not to be abused.

For this woman, as she said in her accompanying letter (appropriately written on the day of her decree absolute), 'The world is my oyster, now!' She has broken through that barrier of pain and worthlessness to find her spiritual self and, just as importantly, is now actively working to help others make that same 'long leap'.

By spiritual I do not mean religious, although the two are often confused, nor do I mean superstition and dogma or otherworldliness. As a Sagittarian, I have always believed that spirituality is 'a personal odyssey', that we are spiritual beings on a human journey, and that life is the search for meaning and purpose – a purpose which must include humour, laughter, love and play because these are a vital part of the human experience. The definitions of spirituality I found most helpful were Theresa King O'Brien's: 'The discovery of what it means to be fully human', and Chandra Patel's: 'Spirituality is understanding reality – the value of life and its meaning – through the everyday experiences of our lives'.[7] I firmly believe that it is in these 'everyday experiences' that women can, and must, express their spirituality. It is not something separate from everyday life, it is Life itself. I also believe that feminine spirituality must start from knowing that, just as our inner spirit resides *in* a living body, so do we reside *on* a living body: the planet earth. Earth is conscious, she breathes, she has her own cycles and she in turn is part of a greater whole. It is this connection with the microcosm and the macrocosm that is, and always was, sacred.

The 'sacred' quality of women's lives has largely been lost in the modern world, but it is possible to retrace it. Interestingly, knowledge of this lost 'knowing' has been incorporated into the 'masculine' symbology of religion, and may well have been part of the esoteric (or hidden) knowledge behind the public face of religion. Many of the old 'Christian' saints were, in fact, the goddess incorporated into a new guise as the early Church found it impossible to eradicate her worship; the 'St Brigid' sites in Ireland being a particular example.

At Chartres cathedral in France, dedicated to the Virgin Mary, there used to be a black madonna and child in the crypt (the one there now is a reproduction). There still is one in the nave. These black madonnas are very ancient and hold the immense power of the feminine within them – Chartres is believed to be built on the Druidic site of 'our Subterranean Lady'[8] – and there is still a holy well below the altar, as in so many English cathedrals. In the nave above the crypt, there is a maze laid out in the form of the sacred vulva of the goddess. Around the cathedral are a group of churches exactly mirroring the constellation of Virgo (the Virgin of the modern zodiac).[9] Aeons ago, Virgo was the sign of fertility: the 'Virgin' was the Corn (or Grain) Maiden who symbolized the birth-death-rebirth cycle and the fruitfulness of the earth. She is a direct link back to the archetypal images explored in Chapter 6.

There are three figures in particular whom I have found most helpful in attuning to the feminine face of spirituality. All are ancient, archetypal, but all are accessible to women today and all are components of the Wise Woman. They are the Crone (Power), the Sybil (Foresight), and Sophia (Wisdom). Activating the goddesses will have helped your contact with these potent figures and the qualities they personify, and they may well have already started to surface in your dreams. However, just as with all the other figures, they can be accessed through active imagination.

THE CRONE IN HISTORY

The Crone, or Hag, was an image which used to be honoured, who had a place and function in society. She was a figure of awe, literally seen as having the power of life and death. She was the grandmother of the tribe, the wise one who guided and inspired. Her wrinkles were a 'badge of honour'.[10] Part of a trinity, she symbolized maturity, authority and inexorable death. As a leader of the tribe, she was the antithesis of patriarchal values, attuned to nature and instinct. Valuing life and its rhythmic cycles, she was equally comfortable with, and unafraid of, death and change. 'A figure of strength, courage and wisdom [Daly] . . . the crone, the sibyl, a woman whom men cannot bind by making pregnant – a woman of power' (Patricia A. Kaufert).[11] And, inevitably, men feared her power. She was that aspect of life that men would most like to control but against which they are powerless: death. The Crone was healer, seer, medicine woman and, when death arrived with inexorable certainty, she was the midwife for the transition to another life.

All of these functions were gradually usurped by men and, in time, even the term 'Crone' became an insult, a denigration of women's wisdom. Equally inevitably, men, in their effort to suppress her power, persecuted and reviled the older woman who was seen, at best, as an inconvenient nuisance and, at worst, a malevolent danger. Throughout history the Crone has been condemned, harassed and hated – by men. Women somehow, despite all the odds, managed to perpetuate the Crone's wisdom and skills down through the centuries. The culmination of the battle, in the west, came in the three centuries of witch hunts. Woman, as a species, has never recovered the power and can barely recall the wisdom that was lost, but the collective memory remains and is calling women to regain their bloodright: feminine power.

With a history like this, it is little wonder that I hesitated to use the term 'Crone' in this book. Searching for an acceptable substitute brought home to me just how powerful the taboo still is against women's power. I settled on 'Wise Women' for the overall concept because this conveyed to me exactly what I was talking about: women's wisdom, knowing, insights, skills, spirituality and, above all, that indefinable aura of power, but all of these qualities belonged to the Crone in days gone by. Even the term 'Wise Woman' had its negative connotations. Some women felt it was too 'airy-fairy', others that it had an esoteric meaning which would put 'ordinary' women off; others thought it was synonymous with the dark forces of witchcraft and superstition, or that it belonged to some strange feminist religion.

Like the dual goddesses, the Crone is a figure who incorporates both dark and light, life and death, creation and destruction, form and dissolution. She acts as a guide through the great passages of life. She is attuned to the natural cycles and rhythms, and as such can be a potent guide to maturity.

POWER

Power is another word with negative connotations because it is open to abuse and misuse, so it is seen as egocentric, manipulative and exploitative: 'power over' rather than 'empowering'. Above all, we are familiar with the destructive side of power. As *Women of a Certain Age* points out, it is a word that belongs to men rather than women. Power is men's motivation, what they actively seek and would kill for. Women, on the other hand, fear power and often refuse to recognize it is a feminine quality. 'From the mythic Medea to the Jungian archetype, power in women is seen as dangerous, destructive, devouring – too fiery, too impassioned, too uncontrolled and uncontrollable to be permitted expression.'[12]

Like the Crone, power has a dual face: most 'matriarchs' acquire 'good', if somewhat diluted, power, but 'witches' and 'feminists' acquire 'bad' power – the qualitative judgement often depending on the observer's point of view. 'Bad' power usually means taking back the projection of assertion or aggression from the convenient male hook on which it has been deposited for most of the woman's life, so that the woman becomes autonomous and powerful in her own right. It is this assertive (or aggressive, depending on your standpoint) attitude which is so noticeable in the so-called 'primitive' societies and yet seems to be so feared in the West.

This fear of acknowledging or owning power is understandable when we look at what marriage during the 1950s and early 1960s usually entailed. It was rare for a woman to continue with her career, childrearing came first. Most women simply transferred their dependence, emotional or financial, from their father to their husband, who was the 'bread-winner' and therefore seen as the powerful person in the relationship. For many, even the ownership of property was male-dominated. In one-parent families, the dependence was often transferred to the Welfare State. No wonder taking up a 'proper' career again in midlife is a threatening event for women (let alone their male partners); it replays all the separation issues that were never psychologically resolved when the woman 'left home'. And even more frightening, then, is the notion of 'owning power'.

I have always found Debbie Boater's definition of power as 'true inner authority, clarity and total freedom'[13] to be helpful in this respect, as this is what happens when you own your power. In other words, you make it your own. 'Owning your own power' is one of those concepts that puzzle people until they have actually done it; then they know what it means. Henry Miller's advice 'not to possess power but to radiate it' seems to sum up how I feel about it. Power is something that *passes through*. It is not *mine*, I am merely the channel through which it flows, and yet it is *mine* in the sense that I choose how to use it and can acquire, and exercise, it through choice.

That notion of choice is vital to the right use of power. Used wisely, power becomes constructive, life-enhancing, empowering. Last night I 'happened' to watch a television programme aptly entitled *The 'Savage' Strikes Back*. It chronicled the struggle of the Innu people of Labrador to regain their land from NATO, who were using it to train pilots in low-level bombing – in the course of which large tracts were devastated and the wildlife seriously affected by the noise pollution. The Innu wanted to go on living on the land in the way their forefathers had always done, rather than move into the settlements provided for them by the government; settlements which encouraged alcoholism and deadness because they had no contact with their lifeblood, the land. According to the, male, Air Force spokesman, there was no conflict. He had no understanding at all of how his activities were affecting the people who lived there – indeed, he kept pointing out that one of the great advantages of this particular part of Labrador was that no one did live there.

What struck me most was one of the women, who was instrumental in the movement to fight for the land and who was imprisoned in the process. This did not, however, dim her spirit. She said that, through the struggle, their women had regained their power. They now knew what women could do. As a result, the Innu have gone back to the land and regained their dignity. Their children are being taught the old ways. They live in harmony with themselves and with nature, taking only what they need to live and acting as stewards for the remainder.

It is this kind of inner power that women need to regain. When power comes from within in this way, its use is directed by the feminine desire to nourish life and it is therefore life-affirming and for the good of all. It recognizes the necessity of death, but it does not actively instigate killing. Like the Crone, feminine power is creator, preserver, and eliminator in the appropriate season.

One of the specific areas where women need to reclaim their power is gynaecology. Women as a whole are aware of how birth, menstruation and menopause have been translated by the, largely, male gynaecologists into a 'disease' from which women suffer. Most women submit to the 'power over' aspect of medicine in that they allow the doctor to have power over their body, accepting what they are told is best for them. The 'healing', such as it is, comes from outside themselves: it is not based on their power to take control of their own bodily processes.

Until HRT came on the scene, hysterectomy was routinely prescribed to cure, or circumvent, the ills of the menopause. Now, HRT has taken over and it may be used to mask emotional 'dis-ease' which would be more rightly seen as a lack of wholeness and balance. Women need to regain the power of choice, power over their body, power to have the knowledge which will lead to the right decision for them. If a woman is in the habit of listening to her body, then she is more likely to have power in this direction. She can also consult her own instinctive and instinctual knowing, the inner figure who is the Crone. And, once she has true knowledge, rather than the superstitious 'old wives tales' and half-truths that often pass for information, she can share this with other women.

EXERCISE
Meeting the Crone

Sit or lie comfortably and close your eyes. Gently breathe out any tension and withdraw your attention into yourself.

When you are ready, picture yourself approaching an ancient forest. A path will open up in front of you, taking you to the heart of the forest.

At the heart of the forest there is a clearing, at the centre of which is an old cottage. There are shafts of sun coming down into this clearing, and the smell of sun-warmed herbs wafts across to you from the garden.

As you arrive, an old lady comes out to greet you. She is the wise old Crone. She invites you into her house and you settle yourself comfortably in a chair.

Spend time with her and ask her to share her wisdom and her experience. Learn from her how to reconcile the paradox of opposites; ask her to take you deep within yourself to the place where her knowing resides.

When you are ready to leave, thank her for being there and ask her to be accessible to you whenever you need her.

Then, leave the cottage and make your way back to the path through the forest, returning to your starting point.

Take deeper breaths and gently return your awareness to the room. Take time to adjust and, when you are ready, open your eyes. Write up your experience in your journal.

This visualization should be repeated from time to time, particularly if the old lady was vague or distant at first. It will gradually become easier to contact her and her wisdom.

THE SIBYL: THE GIFT OF FORESIGHT

Prophecy was much valued in the ancient world and, as with so many other powers, it was either a virgin or a post-menopausal woman who provided the link to the spiritual forces. At Delphi, site of one of the most famous oracles, the Sibyl was originally a young girl, but she was replaced by a woman over fifty. The Delphic Oracle was consulted by kings and commoners, and very little happened in the Greek world without her somewhat ambivalent blessing. This process had value in that it took time to send to the Oracle, time for reflection and reconsideration; and, since her pronouncements were always couched in ambiguous terms, kings, at least, usually did what their instinct told them to do. Instinct is rooted in the collective consciousness, it has its branches in nature and its flowering is intuition.

The ancient Sibyl would sit on the *omphalos*, the mound symbolizing the navel of the world, and there make her prophetic utterances. She was a figure of magic and mystery. However, all post-menopausal women were to some extent believed to have the power of foresight, the ability to peer through the veil that separated the worlds, and so to contact both those who had gone before and what was to come.

The Sibyl is, therefore, a figure of inspiration and intuition. She acts as a mediator between the two worlds: the visible and the invisible, the conscious and the unconscious, the known and the unknown. She is a midwife to the psyche and gives assistance in times of difficult passage, leading a woman into her own inner 'knowing'. I believe that many of the 'symptoms' experienced as part of the menopause are actually an opening up of the intuitive and psychic perception. From my experience of many years of working with people who are opening up to 'other realms', I have found that there are certain 'common denominators', which seem to be particularly active at menopause. 'Symptoms' such as headaches (particularly frontal migraine) or flashes of light, 'tingling' and crawling of the skin (formication), 'giddiness', etc., all occur when this psychic development is taking place. It tends to create a confusion or a sense of 'going mad', particularly when associated with precognitive flashes or a sense of 'going out of time'.

I have long postulated a theory of chemical messengers (carried by the 'wise blood') being involved in both intuition and psychic development, as well as a left brain-right brain fusion, and I feel sure that the hormonal changes of menopause are intended to trigger this expansion into the 'Wise Woman' phase of life. In the past, when women became the seers and holy women, this development would have been encouraged. Unfortunately, with all the witch hunts in historical times, it has been actively discouraged but nature keeps on trying to re-establish the developmental pattern. If a woman can learn to look on this ability as a gift, rather than something evil and cursed, then she can actively utilize this expanded sense of knowing to enhance her own, and others', life: to have her visions and take them out into the community. It is possible to take workshops or classes to open up this intuitive and far-sighted faculty and this will speedily remove the disconcerting 'symptoms'.

The Sibyl often surfaces in dreams and your dream journal may well reveal the intuitive and 'precognitive' aspects of her power. A friend of mine had a characteristic and very powerful dream of meeting a Sibyl in a cave. She was ensconced on a throne formed from a huge python and, in a similar, extremely potent dream, I met a pair of enormous pythons (the female of which was the Sibyl, but she needed her contact with her mate in order to function fully). Pythons, indeed serpents and snakes of all kinds, have long been associated with the Sibyl, who was known as 'the Pythoness' or Pythia at Delphi.

Accessing the Sibyl helps a woman to plan ahead, to foresee what will be, and aids her in using her intuition to guide her life. Intuition takes the separate fragments of what is known and makes a great leap of understanding into a synthesis and a new knowing which is much greater than those parts. It bypasses the logical and rational functioning of the brain to reach a creative solution. This is a feminine gnosis and foresight.

EXERCISE
Meeting the Sibyl

Sit or lie, depending on which is most comfortable. Spend a few moments breathing gently to eliminate tension and to withdraw your attention into your self.

When you are ready, picture yourself standing at the foot of a small valley between two mountains, through which runs a stream. There is a path in front of you. Follow this path up the valley, alongside the stream, until it branches off towards one of the mountains. As you get closer, you will see that the pathway leads to the mouth of a cave.

When you enter the cave, you will see that a path leads down into the mountain. There is a torch to light the way, so take this torch and make your way down to where the Sibyl awaits you.

She is sitting on the *omphalos*, in the centre of a cavern. In front of her is a pool of water. Leave your torch in the bracket by the entrance.

She will motion you to sit by this pool. She may show you, or tell you, all that you need to know to put you in touch with your own foresight, your own sense of prophecy; how to make the link between the seen and the unseen, conscious and unconscious, known and unknown.

When you are ready to leave, thank her and ask her to be accessible to you in the future.

Then pick up your torch and make your way back up to the cave entrance. From here, make your way back down the path to the valley and return to your starting point.

When you are ready to return your awareness to the room, breathe a little deeper, be aware of your body, and then open your eyes. Write up your experience in your journal.

SOPHIA: FEMININE WISDOM

Wisdom, or Sophia, is one of the very ancient concepts. She is very definitely feminine. She dwelt in the 'high places' which were sacred in the old religions, but she is immanent within Christianity – one of her most sacred sites being the sixth century Hagia Sophia church in Istanbul. In some of the older myths, she is the Mother of God, existing before all. In others, she is a co-creator, the feminine soul of God. She has been postulated as the serpent who enticed Eve to eat of the Tree of Knowledge. She is seen as having independent existence, although clearly on the same plane as God, but is actively engaged in relationship with mankind. She is mentioned many times in the Old Testament. In *Proverbs*, for instance, she is portrayed as existing long before the earth:

> Alone, I was fashioned in times long past,
> at the beginning, long before earth itself.
> When there was yet no ocean I was born . . . (8:22–4)

While in *Ecclesiastes* it is said:

> Wisdom raises her sons to greatness
> and cares for those who seek her.
> To love her is to love life; . . .
> To serve her is to serve the Holy One. (4:11–15)

In a similar vein, the *Wisdom of Solomon* says:

> Wisdom . . . is quick to make herself known to those who desire knowledge of her . . . For she herself ranges in search of those who are worthy of her, on their daily path she appears to them with kindly intent, and in all their purposes meets them half way. (6:12–17)

And the writer goes on to chronicle how he called for help at his birth, and the spirit of Wisdom was there. How, throughout his life, he sought her as his bride, and he sets out the gifts that she brings:

> . . . she knows the past, she can infer what is to come, she understands the subtleties of argument and the solving of problems, she can read signs and portents, and can foretell the outcome of events and periods. (8)

But, according to *Ecclesiastes*, Sophia tests those who 'love her'; they have to earn her respect and her gifts:

> At first she will lead him by devious ways,
> filling him with craven fears.
> Her disciples will be a torment to him,
> and her decrees a hard test
> until he trusts her with all his heart.
> Then she will come straight back to him again and gladden
>   him,
> and reveal her secrets to him.
> But if he strays from her, she will desert him
> and abandon him to his fate. (4:17–19)

Sophia then is a Wise Woman, one who epitomizes feminine thought. This thought is of a particular kind. It is 'gestalt' or whole perception; it synthesizes and looks at the overall pattern; it is logical but empathetic, and combines acute observation with intuition. It is relational (taking account of the past in order to project forward into the future), and it arises out of care and concern for man and womankind. It uses both the left and right brain modes of thought. It is creative and concerned with vision and solutions – attributes which are an integral part of the Wise Woman.

LEFT BRAIN-RIGHT BRAIN THOUGHT

It is now well recognized that the different halves of the brain control different functions, and it is beginning to be accepted that each half has its own, different but complementary, way of thinking and perceiving. Each hemisphere experiences reality in its own unique way.

The 'linear' left brain is language-orientated; it is logical, analytic (rather like a computer). It is concerned with reasoning, intellect, sequences, abstraction and categories. It is time-orientated and plans and judges. It can be described as 'masculine' or yang consciousness.

The right brain is non-verbal; it deals in images, metaphors and feelings. This is the seat of the intuition, dreams and ideas; of holistic thought patterns that synthesize simultaneously to make the 'great leap' of insight. It is outside time and, although it has spatial perception, it has no boundaries. This is 'feminine' or yin consciousness.

In a healthy brain, the different modes are connected by nerve fibres running between the two hemispheres, although in most people one or other side of the brain, usually the left, tends to be dominant. However, I believe that, in menopausal women, a synthesis is taking place between the two halves as part of the natural development process. Nevertheless, something may well interrupt the flow between the two halves during this transition phase (the 'chemical messengers' required being triggered by the change in hormone levels, which are of course erratic at first).

One of the common 'symptoms' of the menopause is an occasional 'word blindness'. This is the bizarre sensation that you have 'lost' the word; you know it, you can see it, but you cannot say it – or you say the wrong one. All the time, your hands are making gestures to indicate what you mean – gesture being a right brain activity. This is an indication of the non-verbal communication that the right brain employs to get its ideas across. A simple visual imaging can help to clear this symptom, and to integrate the synthesis of the two halves.

EXERCISE

Close your eyes and relax for a moment.

Take your attention into your brain and scan around it. Notice which side feels larger, more dominant. Which side is neglected?

Notice how the different sides portray a thought. The left brain uses words, clocks, maps, equations, straight lines and symbols. The right brain uses colour, painting, music, dreaming, metaphors, mandalas and spiral patterns.

Now take your attention to the centre of your brain, to the point where the nerve pathway crosses over. See this pathway outlined in light. When it is really strong, imagine that different colours link the right and left, and left and right, sides of the brain. See the coloured lights flashing across, bringing the message to both sides.

It can also be helpful deliberately to choose a right or left brain way of communicating at different times, perhaps experimenting with the opposite function to that usually used. You can use colours and patterns, for instance, to express feelings when the words of the left brain are inadequate. Or, if you are feeling particularly woolly, you can sit down and make lists to activate the left brain. Eventually, you can instinctively choose either or both patterns of thought.

Having worked through this book, you will have activated or strengthened your right brain function but I have found two helpful tools for this work. *Drawing on the Right Side of the Brain*[14] is particularly useful for those who are left-brain dominated and would like to develop their artistic communication, and Matthew Manning's tape 'Creative Visualisation'[15] gives exercises for stimulating both left and right sides, and integrating the two together.

SIGHT AND INSIGHT

Another difficult 'symptom' of midlife which is almost universal (affecting both men and women) is deterioration in eyesight. I have found it helpful to see this as a metaphor for the need to shift to inward sight – to ask Sophia for aid in learning a new way of seeing: literally seeking insight. For the Neo-Platonists, 'blindness' was a pre-condition for seeing God, and many initiation ceremonies use either a blindfold or darkness to symbolize this condition and to focus the initiate on the inner eye of the soul.

Taking time out of each day for meditation, a simple inward focusing of the attention, is an extremely useful way of contacting your inner wisdom. Basically, meditation means reaching a point of inner stillness during which both the mind and body relax. There are many different types of meditation, not all of which are intended for the same purpose – some seek 'enlightenment', others to 'repro-gramme' the mind, for instance. There are also many different ways of meditating. Yoga and T'ai Chi Ch'uan for example, are forms of meditation which involve movement of the body. Others, such as Transcendental Meditation, are performed motionless and use a mantra (a repeated word or phrase) to still the mind. The relaxation exercise in Appendix I can be a useful lead-in to meditation.

Many systems of meditation talk about emptying the mind and this apparent goal can be offputting to those who, like me, have a constant stream of mind-chatter going on. I find, however, that it is possible to acknowledge the chatter but to choose not to be sidetracked by it, and eventually it quietens. If you do have this 'chatter', then using a guided visualization (which involves the mind) will probably be a better choice for you than, for instance, concentrating on the breath or repeating a mantra.

Some people find gazing deeply into a flower or a crystal

is helpful. Others concentrate on a particular colour or build up the picture of a flower, etc., in their mind's eye. Many people are aurally attuned, in which case music can be helpful, or movement-orientated, in which case a discipline like yoga or T'ai Chi would be useful. Other people find half an hour of gardening, swimming or running calms and soothes their mind. Anything which brings you to a point of inner stillness can be used. In the inner stillness, you can then listen to the voice of Sophia bringing you insight and inspiration. She is the source of feminine wisdom.

You may also find it useful to adapt the experience of meeting the Crone or the Sibyl in order to contact Sophia. Remember that she was to be found in the temples built in high places, so go up into the hills to meet her. You can either record this experience in your journal, or draw her to bring the image into reality. Figure 12 shows my Wise Woman, beautifully interpreted for me by my daughter.

Fig. 12   The Wise Woman

Once you have contacted this inner wisdom, you will find that you are stimulated to communicate in a new way: one that has insight and purpose. You may choose to paint or draw, to use words, or to behave in a different way. It may also lead you into a practical expression of your spiritual vision, and it will certainly connect you to your roots as a woman. If these roots are to flower into an ongoing wisdom for all women, then communication between women is vital – particularly so between old and young, mothers and daughters. It is in these contacts that the message of the Wise Woman will have most impact.

MOTHERS AND DAUGHTERS

Nowhere is the taboo of menopause more apparent than between mothers and daughters – and mothers and sons, too, for that matter. I was talking to a well-known actor who, when we were discussing this book, immediately fell into a parody of the 'Oh, poor me' victim role of the menopausal woman which his mother had epitomized for him but never discussed.

If the menopause is to become a natural event, and if women are to identify fully with the cycle of changes which womanhood embodies, then mothers must communicate the whole picture to their daughters. All too often what is known is the 'misery' aspect and, because they have not found it in themselves, mothers are unable to communicate the 'Wise Woman' aspect that follows. The woman who carried out the goddess ritual in Chapter 6 had been closely following the progress of this book, and she suddenly realized that she had never spoken to her mother about this phase of life:

Although obviously I was there when my mother had her menopause, at the time she never talked about it much, so I rang her up and asked: 'Mummy, what happened when you went into the menopause?'

She told me the first sign she thought she had was in fact when she was pregnant at forty. Then it was a long time; she was in her mid-fifties (which she always puts down to having the late baby). She had very few physical symptoms and she didn't suffer from hot flushes, but emotionally she used to get very jittery about everything.

Talking to her about the menopause was the most fantastic experience because although I knew a fair amount about her periods and I knew all about the birth of all of us – she was very open in discussing that kind of thing – the menopause had been something, perhaps at the age I was, being a teenager, she just didn't feel like talking about at the time. I feel that, having talked with her about every other stage, actually going through the whole menstrual cycle and beyond the menopause, it makes a wonderful link between mother and daughter. On a female level, a very close female level, I see that conversation as an important landmark in our relationship because it provided a sense of continuity and intimacy that I think is very important.

Bringing it out into the open makes it something natural, which of course it is, but when nobody talks about these things and shuts them up in the dark, one gets the sense that it is something to be deeply ashamed of, that it's an illness, that it's something dark and something wrong, which it isn't, and it gives you a sense of continuity and connection with other women.

'Going public' with the menopause can be a traumatic experience and one which is sometimes unavoidable, as hot flushes can arise at the most inappropriate times. However, if menopause was seen, and talked about, as a natural event, this 'shamefulness' would be avoided.

Another of my friends is the daughter of Cherry Marshall. Together they used to appear on a British television afternoon programme called 'House Party'. It was an extremely informal setting, women chatting about things of interest to women. There were no experts, just the women themselves, and it was an immensely popular programme. Sarah, Cherry's daughter, has been of tremendous help and encouragement to me in writing this book and, when we were discussing the experience above, she told me about her mother's experience of bringing this menopause into the domain of The Great British Public:

It must have been about twenty years ago that she actually did it on House Party. She talked about her own menopause, and talked about the symptoms, and there was a general conversation about it. It was a bit shocking at the time, it just wasn't talked about, but it generated an enormous amount of mail. Then a month later she was at Heathrow airport, and this woman came rushing up, dragging her husband behind her, and said in a booming voice: 'Oh Cherry, Cherry, I've been longing to talk to you about the menopause. It's started! You should see me, I'm completely drenched at night and what you said about hot flushes. . . .' It cleared quite a space around her and everyone took a good look!

Sarah, however, has grown up believing both menstruation and the menopause to be a perfectly natural part of life. She has that sense of connectedness to womanhood, of continuity, and she expects to move quite naturally into the Wise Woman phase of existence, as her mother has.

MOVING INTO THE WISE WOMAN

This book will have helped you to value yourself for who you are, to connect to your own self and inner wisdom. This will give you the confidence, and the courage, to make changes in your life and to define for yourself your 'Wise Woman' role in society. It will have helped you towards the spiritual pregnancy which will, in due time, come to fruition as the Wise Woman. You may, however, find it inspiring to read one woman's experience of moving into the Wise Woman, of giving birth to her new self:

Birth

It was Me
I was giving birth to,
The throes of Labour
Which seemed so long,
So arduous, so pain-wracked,
Waiting, pacing for the Child
To come.

It was Me
All along,
Who was waiting in the womb.
Me,
Whose creation I was making.

It was Me
Whose expulsion was needed,
Whose bloodied head
Emerged,
Whilst I laughed and cried
With the Joy
Of Me.

It was me,
After all,
Who was the fruit
Of all that agony.
The dilated neck expanding,
Inch by tortuous inch,
To allow the long slithering
Outside the crucible
Of all my panting and screaming,
Contracting and resting,
Resting and contracting,
Wondering how long, how long
Was THIS
Going to take?

Wondering whether it would be all right,
Whether it was a boy or a girl,
Whether it had all its fingers and
toes . . .

And then –
The Creative Force
Pushed Me out,
Great Muscles
Called together great effort
And expelled me, black and blue,
Streaked with water, blood and fat,
A newborn wailing, waving, saving
Me, Myself, I AM–

And All Creation Sang Itself
In Me.

Shirley Clark

In a long covering letter to me, Shirley (who has also
worked with many women of menopausal age and who
has just completed her own menopause) gave me the benefit
of her thoughts on the menopause, much of which I had

already covered in this book. It was interesting how we had both come, independently, to the same conclusions and used the same images. I feel that this 'knowing' is something all women share on an inner level. Also, having completed her transition. Shirley was the one woman who wanted to be acknowledged by name. It was the culmination of owning her power. She explained the background to her experience of re-birthing herself:

> We need, during this period of necessary change, to see ourselves as transforming and re-forming ourselves. To do this, I believe, we need to go back, through creative visualizations, through counselling where it is needed, to our own half-remembered childhoods. There we will find the 'inner child' we were born to be – the spiritual being that came into the world to take part in the gradual awakening of all humankind. And to become the Grand Mother of the present Time.
>
> Having done this work on myself, I found that I had to 'give birth' to Myself. Having given birth to real live children, the time had come for me to rebirth myself, spiritually and psychologically. I had to find the Inner Feminine in myself and the Inner Masculine and have these two principles give rebirth to my originally created Self, the 'Wonder Child' of my own True Self.
>
> In order to find the Creative Spirit in myself, I had to go back to the child I once was to find her Soul's purpose for being here now . . . There, in my childhood, I found that there were footprints that I had yet to follow. I had an experience of seeing it as if there was virgin snow and my footprints had not yet made their unique mark. In this way, I believe that all women can find their own particular pathways during and after the 'Pause' in their lives [menopause] whilst they re-assess their lives and the meaning of their lives in the present, perhaps even as spiritual awakening for others.
>
> Having come through the Inner Marriage of our inner feminine (creative receiving wisdom) and inner masculine (active dynamic love) we can truly come into our own. We must Midwife ourselves into this New Birth. It is an actual experience when it happens, and like all births requires a period of carrying, of burden, of heaviness, of parturition, and of pain, of bleeding, of the long dark tunnel within ourselves, spiritually a very dark time – the dark night of the soul – and of the Joy of Birth.

This Birth, or Re-Birth, is in some senses a deeply sexual act. It is a moment of fullness, and it is a fruition of ourselves.

When we link up with our original child self and hold hands, as it were, into the Present with our present day self, we can discover that all our experiences throughout our lives have contributed to and given us Wisdom. The 'Sophia' upon which the universal principle of creation is founded. We are a part of the Foundations of the Earth.

Each woman must come to the Wise Woman phase in her own way, and express the energy in her own unique experience of life. She will be attuned to the natural rhythms and she may choose to utilize art, music, writing, dance or theatre to communicate her wise self, or close and intimate contact with others. Some women are drawn to women's groups, perhaps for self help initially, maybe to practise rituals or spirituality. Women may choose to enter politics or law, either at a local, national or international level, fighting for the human rights of everyone. They may do this quietly, one to one; or go out to meet the world and pass on feminine gnosis. The Wise Woman may well form part of an extended 'family' group whose bond is spiritual essence rather than conventional blood ties, although they will be bound together by the shared feminine experience of wise moon blood – spirituality leads to a sense of community and connection with all creation.

Women may meet resistance, not least from themselves, but if a woman has courage and perseverance and sees the setbacks as a strengthening of her resolve, then she will win through. There are few positive role models. But we can learn from what has gone before, and we can group together to discuss and help each other. At no other time in the recent historical past have women had so much to build on, and such a potential for expressing their power. For instance, many of the young women from the Greenham Common Peace Camp in England have now reached, or are approaching, the menopause. Similarly, the 'Mothers Against Vietnam' campaign in the States, whose motto was 'War is unhealthy for children and other living things', was supported by women who are now of mature years. These women know how to campaign for change and recognize the power of the group.

In a pertinent article[16] written in July 1991, Maureen Freely pointed out how far from the 'sharing, caring Nineties' we had already 'progressed'. As she said, the headlines over the past eighteen months had all been of disasters, war and fighting – whether for territory or rights. As she says, they would have been better designated the 'Nasty Nineties'. And yet, she points out, 'We came close to pulling off the media coup of the century. When I say "we", I'm talking about my generation. The so-called counterculture that has been underground, and longing not to be, for a good 20 years now. I sincerely believe that if we had had a few more months of peace and affluence, we could have talked ourselves back into fashion. This time last year we were already well on our way to convincing people, even serious people who ought to have known better, that communism was dead, capitalism doomed, . . . it was just a question of translating these ideas into compelling visual images.' As she points out, 'Vietnam did not stop people calling it "the Swinging Sixties" . . . because flower power made more enjoyable television than the Tet offensive.' And she asks: 'Isn't it too early in the decade to give up hope of remaking it in our image? Why don't we give it one more try?'

It is not just a question of translating it into images, although these can be potent symbols. It is a question of sincerely wishing to make it work. This is the task of the Wise Woman.

Other women are recognizing the immense power an individual woman has as a consumer. The plan to boycott Nescafé, for instance, until Nestlé stop distributing 'free' powdered milk to Third World countries and the move towards 'dolphin-safe tuna' show what can be done. If women simply stop buying products that are environmentally unfriendly or health hazards, then manufacturers will have to listen. It is not necessary to be strident or extreme in order to bring about change.

As Nor Hall has pointed out,[17] man is now as dependent on fossil fuel as the ancient hunter was upon deer. The concerns of that hunter were his own physical survival, and whether the resources would hold out. The recent Gulf War has shown that the fear is still the same, and man's answer is to fight, to try to gain power through possession. However, woman could have another answer: find a different way to use the resources we have. In England, for instance, the burning of straw in fields has now been banned. A farmer remarked on a recent television programme that the manufacturer who could find a way to compress straw into usable fuel (after all, they have the same base) would make a fortune. It is women who could press for, and carry out, this kind of research. We can follow the advice to 'walk lightly over the earth' who is our mother.

Similarly, in England again, the number of school leavers has dropped drastically and employers are finally realizing that they will have to woo the older woman, to utilize that vast pool of skills and resources that they have ignored for so long. Women can press for training, for grants, for the other facilities they need, to enable them to return to education or work and make full use of their innate managerial and organizational talents. They can also identify ways to employ themselves, to market their own individual and unique talents and creations to fill an unrecognized niche. This pathway of independent self-employment is a hard but rewarding one and it could be extended into 'cooperative' groups of women, each contributing according to need and ability.

Women have always been the backbone of the voluntary sector, no charity could function without them, and women who have financial security could extend this kind of help – particularly into the less fortunate areas of the world. So much expertise is needed; the planet is crying out for a proper sharing of resources between countries and individuals. Even within one's own country there are many fields, counselling or care for instance, where there are simply not enough people to help the troubled. Experienced women could also act as mentors, passing on their knowledge and skills in the old way. They could prepare the young for womanhood, and then help them to become Wise Women in their turn.

Men had to listen when the feminist movement demanded rights. Now perhaps it is time for the feminists (and everyone else) to listen to what 'ordinary women' want and need (although, in my opinion, all women are extraordinary). So, women must come together to formulate exactly what it is they do want from life and what they can, in turn, contribute to life.

As Shirley Clark has pointed out: 'We can encourage men in their own search for themselves, so that the balance between the masculine and the feminine may come into being, both personally and universally. Then, men and women who are willing to do so can work together, sharing their discoveries and insights into spiritual and personal growth, and in so doing help the healing of the planet.'

We 'ordinary women' can decide whether to accept the standards of youth and beauty that have prevailed, or whether to wear our wrinkles with pride and give up our diets – to allow our inner being to shine through and to be truly ourselves. We have a choice and the power to carry that choice through. No longer can we wait passively for someone else or hope that time will make the changes; the menopause signals that the time for change is Now. When I asked singer and ardent feminist Julie Felix what difference the menopause had made to her, she reflected a moment and then said, 'I have stopped looking forward to the next green field. I have started living in the Now'.

As Honora Lee Wolfe, the author of *Second Spring*, has pointed out:

> As a group now coming into power, we have the possibility to make history, to halt environmental degradation, to tame technology for peace and humanity, and to reintegrate our culture and thereby ourselves . . .
>
> I believe that my generation of women can be, indeed must be, a major part of those solutions if indeed solutions are to be found. By so doing, we may find a second spring, the strength and purpose that we need to live whole and healthy through the menopause and beyond.[18]

Maybe now we can join suffragist Eliza Farnham who, in the 1860s, saw the menopause as a 'time of secret joy, spiritual growth, and super-exaltation'. As Jesus is reputed to have said, 'Not to join in the dance is to mistake the occasion'. The dance is the dance of life, with its interweaving rhythms and natural cycles, and the occasion is the celebration of who you are – now. The Wise Woman is uniquely placed to live life to the full, 'to dance it' as she moves lightly over the earth.

RITES OF PASSAGE

Rites of passage are deeply secret and jealously guarded, passed on from generation to generation, and it may be that no records have survived for menopausal rites. Certainly it would seem that when a woman became 'the holy woman', this would be marked by a ceremony. In some American Indian tribes, for instance, the event of menopause was marked by the woman moving into the 'Grandmother Lodge' where, free from chores, she was able to dream her visions to enrich the community.[19] In parts of Greece today, the older women still participate in the death rites in exactly the same way they did over 2000 years ago when the Eleusinian mysteries were the source of spiritual sustenance.

Rites of passage were undertaken at significant times, not only to mark out the importance of the event but also to bring the blessing of the gods and goddesses into the community at a crucial stage of life. Rites of passage are, therefore, a link with the spiritual forces which the so-called 'primitive' person sees as pervading life. They are an extension of the small rituals we all use every day: touching wood, for instance, wards off the dark powers by counter-acting the hubris that follows on an unthinking assumption of good fortune. Throwing salt over your shoulder placates the gods. Ritual has an inner meaning, it is something private and internal. When viewed from outside, it is merely an enactment (or re-enactment) of a drama. Viewed from inside, it is the power of life itself.

Creating your own rite of passage could be the key to opening up your future as a Wise Woman, particularly if you have activated all the energies of the feminine within yourself and integrated these with the masculine, bringing about a true synthesis and wholeness. One woman, for instance, threw a 'Menopause Party' and invited all her friends to join her in a ritual burning of sanitary protection to celebrate her release. Another wrote a poem; yet another went off to Greece on her own to 'commune with the ancient energies'. The possibilities are endless!

Rites of passage have three stages. In the first, the initiate withdraws from society and spends a period of time in isolation, communing with herself. This is followed by the 'ordeal' phase in which some test or symbolic renunciation is acted out. And finally, after renewal and rebirth, there is the re-emergence into the community. If you have performed the 'Rite of Mourning' from Chapter 4, you have undertaken the first stage, and this chapter will have helped you with the second. All that remains then is to celebrate your re-entry into the community as a Wise Woman.

EXERCISE

At an appropriate time, create a ritual for your menopausal rite of passage and act this out.

THE MENOPAUSE MANDALA

When I came to full realization of what the menopause meant to me, I found that it was helpful to describe my attunement to what was happening in my body. I created a 'menopause mandala'. The mandala arose spontaneously out of a body workshop weekend, despite the block I have always had with drawing. I found that, when I stopped struggling with the concept of 'drawing', the mandala created itself on paper the colour of old blood. In subtle, gentle yet glowing pink and coral tones, a joyful ammonite-form shaped itself on the paper, beautifully describing the cycle of active and passive energies I was experiencing, spiralling around a crimson 'wise blood' centre. I framed it and hung it on my study wall. It has been a source of inspiration during the writing of this book, reminding me that I can travel inward to the centre of my being to commune with myself, or outward to communicate the insights I gain there to the outside world.

EXERCISE

Have ready to hand paper and paint, pastels or crayons. Then close your eyes and spend a few minutes quietly focusing on your breathing. When you are relaxed, allow an image to form which symbolizes your menopause.

You may need to begin drawing before you have a clear image, trusting that it will come and allowing your hands to translate the inner knowing of your body onto the paper. Alternatively, it may appear full blown on the inner screen of your mind. You may find that words come; maybe a poem to express your feelings or a joyful celebration of who you are. When you have finished, frame your creation and hang it prominently so that it will remind you that the changes you are experiencing are purposeful and have meaning.

CONCLUSION

Life After Menopause

The post-parental woman is energized to seek out, to take advantage of, and even to create the powerful roles that fit her expanded energies and new appetites.[1]

David Gutmann

Having made the transition through the menopause, many women find that they have new energy, a zest for life which is unstoppable. The energy empowers them quite literally into a new way of being.

When I was collecting women's stories about the post-menopause phase, I found so many that were inspiring. Many of them turned what seemed to be a tragic end into a creative new beginning. One such story was Anne's.

Anne was married for twenty five years. The wife of a successful businessman, she had given up her singing career to look after him and his children from his first marriage. As she approached fifty, her husband began an affair with a younger woman, for whom he eventually abandoned the marriage. It was a long and painful process for her.

Finally alone, she was disorientated, having devoted herself to his needs for all those years. Tentatively at first, she began to sing a little once again, mainly for herself, then for family and close friends. She began to gain confidence and eventually gave a small recital locally, which was well received.

Around this time she 'coincidentally' began to have a passionate affair with the son of a friend of hers, then in his late twenties.

Five years have now passed. Her singing career proceeds from strength to strength, and she is still happily involved with her young lover.

I asked several of the older, Wise Women I knew what difference the menopause had made to them. For almost all of them, it was a turning point. One, who has just had her eightieth birthday but whose energy and appetite for life remains undiminished, replied that she was certain that 'the menopause frees one to become more spiritual and to serve the world from this orientation':

> Certainly, in my own life I am aware of three moments of spiritual awakening which coincided with a change in my mundane workspace, each of which took place at the end of August – the time of my birth under Virgo.
>
> The first was a move to Leicester University's Institute of Education in 1957 at the age of forty-seven. This is where I first met Mary Swainson, serving the Psychological Counselling Service, provided by its Department of Education. We recognized our mutual commitment immediately and started working together. We were soon joined by the group which included Ruth White and Gildas (a discarnate spiritual teacher), whose work is recorded in *Gildas Communicates*.
>
> The second was a move to Northumberland to establish and develop a new College of Education for students being educated for teaching. From the beginning I was able to recruit teaching staff in sympathy with my philosophy, which filtered through to the students they were teaching. There was a Quiet Room on the campus used by staff and students and by what had become known as the Gildas Group.
>
> During this time also, summer schools on spiritual subjects were arranged by me, every year, during the college vacations. These included Sir George Trevelyan (founder of The Wrekin Trust, a 'spiritual education' organization).
>
> The third was at the moment of my retirement in 1976 at the age of sixty-five to a village in north Northumberland which I had been told three years previously by my spiritual guide would be my retirement home. Shortly after I arrived, The Northumbria Seekers was born.
>
> During this time I have been attending the Transpersonal Psychology workshops and also the training workshops. These experiences have deepened my appreciation of my spiritual potential and informed my work as a psychotherapist.
>
> Some time ago, I was asked if I could find time to write my autobiography. My answer was No – I'm far too busy!

One of the wonderful things that emerged from my research was that it is never too late. Many women began to train for new 'careers' when they retired or when their children left home; others picked up their old, neglected, talents, as in the case of the singer mentioned above. Other women simply got on with their lives, but brought a new energy and enthusiasm to bear. All, in their own way, became Wise Women.

One such woman is the friend to whom this book is dedicated. She, more than any other person, convinced me that life after menopause has both purpose and joy and, over the years, she has taught me the real meaning of change. Her story illustrates what can be achieved by mature women, and also just how many beginnings and endings life has. She has always struck me as a deeply spiritual person and I asked her when her own spiritual development began:

> I suppose I started meditating when I was pre-menopausal. It was during a big change, when my husband left me – I was forty-eight. Then I moved house and the day of the move, which was absolutely horrendous, I had my last period. Everything except the period was diabolical because it snowed and one of the removal vans did not turn up, someone heaved a stone through the window so I had to have the police. We also had a fire and a flood so it was really quite dramatic!
>
> I had gone back to work part-time because I still had school age children, and when we moved house I realized I was getting very bored. I started reflex zone therapy because I needed to do something more, something different. The children were making all kinds of teenage demands and I was getting no support from my other half, so life was very difficult. Then, when I was fifty-seven, I was offered a full-time job to start up a whole new project, which was a wonderful beginning when I had been thinking 'All I have to do is sit here until I'm sixty and then get out as fast as I possibly can'. In fact, this job went on into my mid-sixties when I decided to 'retire' and work part-time again. Then I moved once more – I move house regularly – and life was changing again.
>
> I suppose what was happening was that I was realizing that being a parent, being a physio, being all these other things, was *what* I was and what I really needed to find out was *who* I was. The meditation helped on that, it was the start of me realizing, but I had found it a little bit airy-fairy sometimes. It was wonderful but it was not a world I could live in. You could escape from the trauma but it was not to do with living with the trauma, not the way I wanted to.

So I started a three-year psychosynthesis training, which was an in-depth course and an enormous learning about myself. It grounded a lot of the meditation stuff and it was really a learning of who I was, although I still don't know completely. It's finding out who I am, and finding out who I am changes my relationship with other people, makes it better, much more real. And it also makes me feel more comfortable with things that I used to run away from, and things that I didn't like, and that doesn't mean that I still don't get into a state, get angry. In fact, I possibly show my anger much more than I ever did before so life is much more real for me now. People are much more real. I don't judge them nearly so easily and therefore relationships with people are much more fun.

What I want to do is to go on discovering who I am; I want to practise psychosynthensis, I want to work with people who have auto-immune illnesses, and children, but really whatever comes up.

I was never frightened of dying but I'm much more comfortable about it now. You are born, you die, and you need to know how you feel about dying, just as you need to know when you are alive how you feel about living. I think when you think about dying, then you are much more likely to live than you are if you simply don't think about it. There's no urgency in living but there's just, for me, a need to live fully.

Always active and dynamic, over the years I have watched her increase in confidence as she found herself. To me, she epitomizes the Wise Woman. What she did not mention was that, towards the end of her sixties, she had a schedule which would exhaust a much younger woman. She regularly commutes to London in order to counsel others and to continue her own self-exploration. She has just finished a challenging AIDS counselling training and has finally given up her part-time employment in order to become a self-employed therapist. And, once again, she is hoping to move house.

As I believed that feeling confident at the menopause was closely tied up with women's perceptions of themselves and how they view 'middle age', I spoke to Cherry Marshall, now in her late sixties but still exceptionally fit and well with tremendous vitality. Cherry had a modelling school for twenty five years but has always been interested in 'ordinary' women – back in the 1960s she ran a grooming course for 'older women'. She says that, at that time, it was women in their thirties who considered themselves 'older women'. Cherry still runs the course today but now it is women in their mid-forties and upwards who come to learn how to make the best of themselves. She often gets 'middle-aged' women ringing up about the courses who ask 'Am I too old?' and says that what they are really asking is 'Am I too old to bother about myself?' Cherry feels that any woman, no matter what her age, can learn to make the most of, and, more importantly, feel good about, herself.

Looking good as you mature seems to depend on adapting your style to suit how you look now rather than trying to recapture lost youth. It is no use pretending the years are not going by. What was suitable in your twenties will tend to look ridiculous in your forties and fifties, whereas a style that suits your personality and your age will help you to feel good about yourself. There is no need to be 'fuddy-duddy' and old-fashioned. If you have the courage to try clothes in new designs and colours, this can work wonders for your confidence and many of the fluid, stretchy fabrics add considerably to your level of comfort so that you appear to be relaxed and at ease. And, as Cherry points out, how you move will considerably affect how other people perceive you. If you move as though you are carrying the burden of age, you will appear old, but moving with grace and lightness conveys an impression of vitality. Heavy make-up is ageing, but light make-up skilfully applied can enhance your appearance considerably.

Cherry has noticed that the forty-five year olds want to keep up to date, but that many of the fifty and over age group are actually terribly depressed. They are deeply in the middle of menopause and it is closely related to how their husbands look at them. Cherry finds, for instance, that she has quite a struggle with women who desperately want to look better but who are afraid to go home, for instance with light eye make-up, 'because of what their husbands will say'. She points out that husbands hardly ever notice, except to say how nice their wives look. For Cherry, making the best of oneself does not mean trying to look young or holding back the years:

Whatever age you are, or whatever group you are in, that's the age you are. Feel good about it. I impress this all the time. And it's all tied up with a woman's attitude to ageing because we are so influenced by what we see on television and magazines; the role image is for beautiful young girls.

If you feel good about yourself, you will look good. It is the general aura and vitality that count.

Cherry strongly believes in the power of positive thought and says, 'It is unfortunate that the menopause coincides with getting older!' She recognizes the need for good role models and points to the French women who believe that 'as they get older they accumulate sexuality, they think it grows, even when they've gone through the menopause. They think of themselves as sexual and fully capable, and so it comes through in their personality'.

It was Cherry's daughter who first told me briefly the 'never too late' story which led me to look on Cherry as a transformer. She was advising on a television programme for women over sixty-five, and became particularly involved with one of the women who had become psychologically 'stuck' in the menopause phase, even though physically she had long passed it, because of her own ideas. In Cherry's words:

She was a Jamaican woman of about sixty-five, possibly a little older, her husband had died and she lived with her family, and she hadn't been out of the house for years. She had been a very good dressmaker but she stopped because she thought she was out of touch so she didn't make anything, even for herself.

When she came on the programme, she was absolutely lovely and I chose clothes for her that were very different from the type of clothes she normally wore, although she was a smart woman who had style. I put her in colours she had never worn. . . . Mainly I was saying to her how lovely she looked; she had wonderful hair and very smooth skin, so I wanted her to recognize that.

She had never had any attention paid to her and when she came in the next day she could not believe it, her daughters and the next door neighbours had come in to see her to ask what was going on, why was she on television, etc. She told me that she had never talked so much; she realized that they thought there must be something very special about her, and she had never felt special.

I had three days with her. The most exciting thing was that the people who were in the programme then had to go for aromatherapy, etc., and they had to meet at Waterloo station. The camera crew picked them up and they had the shock of their lives. There was this woman; they didn't recognize her at first, not only had she made an exact copy of one of the outfits I had chosen for her, she had been practising walking because she wanted to look as good as she felt, and she said: 'It has changed my life. I have already told people I'm going to make clothes for them – I know what they like, I recognized immediately what you were telling me. I'm going to start classes, and I'm going out'.

She commented that she had wasted fifteen years and she said: 'It was all in my mind, nobody locked me in, nobody made me give up anything, it was me'.

It is stories like this which have been my inspiration for writing this book. Like Cherry, I believe in positive role models and I am fortunate in having friends who do express the positive, Wise Woman role very actively in their lives. One of these friends is singer Julie Felix, who has always had more than a touch of the Wise Woman about her, but who found that the menopause years widened her spiritual understanding. Her post-menopausal vision of woman in the totality of her experience can inspire us all:

> Woman, sweet like summer corn
> You're a woman
> To the Goddess you were born
> Beautiful Woman
> Sweet sister of mine
>
> You serve the old
> You raise the young
> You caught the stars when they were
> flung into the sky.
> You heal the sick
> You feed the poor
> It is your love that lights the way and that's
> for sure – 'cause you're a
>
> Woman, . . .
>
> Your scars are deep
> Your tears are warm
> It is your thread that mends the sails

when they are torn.
And like a wave
Your heart may break
But it keeps pounding like the sea
make no mistake – 'cause you're a

Woman, . . .

Isis, Astarte, Diana, Asteroth
Tell us of the mysteries that we forgot
Virgin, girl child, madonna and old crone
The faces of the Moon
They let you know
You're not alone
You're a woman, raped and cheated for so long
You're a woman, to the goddess you belong
Beautiful woman, sweet sister of mine

And from the moon
We'll gather light
Illuminate the dark, take back the night
You channel love
And love is strong
And you'll regain your rightful place before too long

Woman, . . .

You're a woman
Pure like winter snow
You're a woman
And it's time for you to know
That you are strong
And you've got power
You're getting stronger
By the hour
And like a flower, you need rain
And when it rains it pours
I'm a sister of yours

I'm talking to you,
Woman, sweet like summer corn
You're a woman
To the goddess you were born
Beautiful woman
Sweet sister of mine.[2]

APPENDIX I

DETOXIFYING DIET

Breakfast:	Cooked, pre-soaked dried fruit including apricots, peaches, pears, figs, prunes, apples. (Note: cooked fresh apples can be included.)
Lunch:	Homemade vegetable soup, or steamed vegetables with brown rice.
Supper:	Brown rice with steamed or, occasionally, stir-fried (using olive oil) vegetables.
Drink:	Drink as little as possible; mineral water or herb teas only. No tea, coffee or alcohol.
Do not use:	Anything you are allergic to. Avoid sugar, salt, bread, dairy foods, tomatoes, citrus fruit, raw foods – fruit should be cooked.
Note:	Brown rice can be cooked with garlic and a little fresh ginger. Herbs can be added to soups and vegetables for flavouring. Tahini paste (rich in calcium) can be thinned with water to make a sauce for occasional use.

Follow the strict diet for 2–4 weeks, then gradually introduce non-allergic foods again, stopping immediately if an adverse effect is noticed. Symptoms may get worse before they get better as the detoxifying process gets under way, but within two weeks the condition should have improved dramatically. An added benefit can be a weight loss of about 7lbs in the first week or two, without any hunger pangs.

RELAXATION EXERCISE

Ensure that you will not be disturbed for the length of time you wish to relax. If you are constrained by time and would worry about how much time has passed, a timer can be used to indicate when the period has elapsed. However, the timer should have a *quiet* tone; being roughly jolted out of relaxation is uncomfortable and counterproductive. Suitable music can help with relaxation and can be used to time the session.

Sit or lie comfortably, preferably in loose clothing. The exercise can either be taped, leaving pauses where appropriate, or memorized (it can be helpful to have a friend read it to you for the first few sessions).

EXERCISE

Have your eyes open to begin with, slowly closing and opening them on each number as you count backwards from ten to one. This will relax your eyelids and, when you have finished the count, you can close your eyes and leave them closed until the end of the session.

Notice how relaxed your eyelids feel, how they lie softly against the bottom lid. Then allow this feeling of relaxation to spread across your forehead and face. If you are aware of any tension, screw up your face and then let it go. If your scalp feels tight, raise and lower your eyebrows to release the tension.

Allow the feeling of relaxation to flow down into your neck and shoulders. If your shoulders feel tight, contract, raise and lower them to release the tension.

Be aware of your arms as the waves of relaxation move down them. Clench and unclench your fists to release the tension, then allow the relaxation to move right down into your fingertips until your arms lie loose beside you.

Allow the feeling of relaxation to flow down into your chest, taking a few deep, slow breaths and breathing out any tension you may be aware of. Then allow the feeling of peace and relaxation to move down into your diaphragm, sensing it soften and relax as you breathe.

Move your breath down into your belly and breathe out any tension you may feel there. Your belly should be relaxed; let it hang out.

Be aware of your hips and lower back and allow the relaxation to flow through them. If there is any tension, contract the buttocks and then let go.

Allow the waves of relaxation to move down into your legs and feet. To free any tension, pull the knees downwards to tighten and contract, and then release. Pull the feet up and then relax. The sense of peace and relaxation should then flow right down to your toes.

Now check that your whole body is feeling loose and relaxed.

Allow your breathing to slow still further, letting the abdominal muscles do the breathing for you and taking a pause between each in- and outbreath. Let yourself be still for a few minutes enjoying this sense of total relaxation and peace. (If you wish to do a short relaxation, the session can terminate here – in which case move to the final instructions ★★.)

As you continue to breathe in a sense of peace and relaxation, become aware that you are surrounded by light. Breathe this light into your heart, feeling it fill and energize.

When your heart is full of light, let it spill out and flow up to your head and down to your feet. Continue to gently breathe in more and more light and let it flow through your body, washing away any pain, stiffness and worries. When you are completely full of light, simply relax and enjoy the sensation of absolute peace.

★★When you are ready to end the session, begin to breathe a little deeper and become aware of the weight of your body once more. Your body will, however, remain relaxed and free from tension. Slowly count from one to ten, by which time you will be wide awake and very alert. Open your eyes and return your attention to the room.

If you wish to fall asleep after this exercise, simply omit the final instructions from ★★ and substitute the following:

Continue to breathe rhythmically, allowing your breathing to deepen until you drift gently into sleep. You will sleep for as long as you wish, waking refreshed and full of vitality.

APPENDIX II

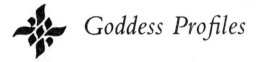 *Goddess Profiles*

THE MATRONS

HERA

The myth

Hera is the sister-wife of the head of the Greek pantheon, Zeus, and the goddess of marriage, although her own marriage appears to have been far from happy. Zeus had been married many times previously and was the arch-philanderer. The Greek myths are full of his adultery and consequent offspring – and Hera's legendary jealousy and rage. According to myth, poor Hera did not have a happy childhood either as she was a child of Rhea and Cronos, and was swallowed by her father as soon as she was born. She was only liberated years later when her brother Zeus, who had escaped being swallowed by the substitution of a stone, was able to overthrow his father and force him to disgorge his children.

However, there is some evidence to suppose that Hera was in fact a much older goddess, a remnant of the Great Goddess who was worshipped prior to classical Greece and who was incorporated into the pantheon by virtue of her convenient marriage to Zeus. In any event, in Hera's recorded early mythological life she was overshadowed by her father, to whom she had handed over her power. Nevertheless, Hera was not a weak woman. When Zeus tried to seduce her, she would not succumb and forced him to marry her. The honeymoon is said to have lasted for 300 years.

However, it would seem that once again she handed over her power. Although Hera was a being of great beauty and virtue, Zeus was not faithful for long and the myths are full of the fights that resulted. On one memorable occasion, Zeus is said to have tied an anvil to each of Hera's ankles, bound her hands, and suspended her from the sky. Hera was no angel, though; she wreaked vengeance on more than one rival for Zeus's attentions and her vindictive temper was chronicled by Homer in the *Iliad*. On more than one occasion it was all too much for her, and she withdrew into solitude. When it became clear that she would not return, Zeus used her jealousy to trick her into submission by enacting a 'marriage' with a local princess. Hera, who was not prepared to give up her position as consort of the head god, is said to have been amused by his trick and decided to stay – the kind of face-saving at which she excelled. Almost all her fits of rebellion somehow backfired on her. In a fit of pique over Athena's 'virgin' birth by Zeus, she herself gave birth, without the aid of a man, to the terrible Typhon, a scourge for mankind.

The archetype

The Hera-woman is first and foremost a wife, a paragon of domestic virtue. She yearns for the prestige and status that marriage, in her eyes, confers. Almost always, within the home, she is 'She who must be obeyed', the dominant matriarch and the backbone of many charitable institutions. Like Hera before her, she will put up with a great deal in order to retain her position – even to the extent of turning a blind eye to her husband's infidelity or addiction so long as she remains 'The Wife'. When she is aware of the affair, she blames the other woman, not her husband.

In many instances she has also handed over her power to her husband. She is the 'power behind the throne', supporting and urging her husband ever onward and upward on the power ladder. And yet the Hera-woman is jealous of his power and his mobility, which she wants for herself but does not know how to get.

In Hera-women who have made their way in the world, the male side dominates. They are ruthless, confident, arrogant and always know best, and their sterile creations may well become the scourge of the world.

The Hera shadow is the jealousy, possessiveness and vindictive temper which Hera could display only too well. But this is based on her inner feeling of powerlessness, of incompletion unless she has a mate, and her fears of loss of self that would result if she was alone. Many of the strident feminists who sought to replace men were reflecting the Hera shadow, as are the highly successful, man-gutting business-women and female politicians who strive to dominate their world.

Unconscious attunement to the Hera archetype may equate with refusing the midlife rite of passage that would link what a woman has been with what she may be. Part of the Hera shadow may be a reluctance to move forward, to change or to grow;

trying instead to cling to the past and 'how it was'. Such a woman cannot face up to the loneliness, and the challenge, of developing a sense of independent self. But, as Nor Hall points out, there is an 'inevitability of the often lonely passage that stretches one beyond "an initiation and a terminus I cannot name" (Robert Duncan)'.[1]

Society has singularly failed the Hera-woman. Her values are no longer the norm, her security is at risk, and her power, which she so needs to own, is not valued. The lack of a socially defined role for the older woman strikes most lethally at the heart of the Hera-woman. She is the one who most misses a rite of passage which would validate her existence, the woman who most needs a sense of continuity to unite past and future so that they meet in the present.

Hera's strongest quality is commitment and her greatest potential is to own her own power and become a woman in her own right.

HESTIA

The myth

Hestia is the goddess of the hearth. The elder sister of Hera and Zeus, she shared Hera's fate of being swallowed by her father but, unlike Hera, when disgorged she actively reclaimed power over her life and refused to hand it over again. Having declined the courtship of both Poseidon and Apollo, she chose instead to remain a virgin and tend the fire at the heart of every home.

She took little part in Olympian mythological life, but was much venerated by the Greeks as her sacred fire made any place holy (that is, the spirit of the god or goddess dwelt there). Hestia is linked to the Vestal Virgins in Rome who tended the sacred flame. At around the age of forty, the virgin priestesses had to choose whether to remain in the temple and instruct the younger priestesses or go out into the world again and carry their spirituality with them, so there is a strong connection between Hestia and the midlife transition.

The archetype

Hestia is virgin, intact. She does not need a man to make her complete, although she may choose to share her life with one. She is the Wise Woman with an inward-seeing eye and a quiet tranquillity that nothing disturbs. She represents harmony and order and exists in the housewife, or any woman, who enjoys her work for the sake of the task itself, being present in the moment.

The Hestia-woman is far more likely to be quietly pursuing the spiritual pathway than climbing the career ladder. In Hestia-woman in whom devotion to spiritual matters has been outwardly unapparent for the first half of life, a change will come about at the midlife point and their spiritual leanings will become more defined and urgent.

Detachment is one of Hestia's qualities and this may lead to the shadow of a woman who appears unaware of the needs of others, seemingly cold and uncaring because of her inwardly focused self. It may also lead to the 'wishy-washy' type of spiritual woman, commonly found in ashrams and communities, whose attention is so inwardly focused that she is incapable of managing out in the world. Or to the celibate who has renounced sexuality, finding virtue in repression, and who equates 'virgin' with 'untouchable' rather than the old meaning of 'intact and whole'.

The Hestia shadow can also be present in the woman who 'serves others' from a sense of no-self, a lack of inner value and worth; or from a sense of moral superiority and a kind of inverted snobbery; or the 'religious' woman who serves the letter of the law rather than its intent and who imposes her own morality and judgement on others in the certainty that she knows what is good for them.

Unattached to people or outcome, the positive Hestia-woman is centred in herself and offers a wise perspective with which to view the world. In her role of keeper of the hearth, she is the centre that nourishes others from her resource of spiritual power. She has inner light and a strong connection to her self which gives her the potential to be a truly Wise Woman.

MAIDEN AND MOTHER

DEMETER AND PERSEPHONE

The myth

Demeter is the corn goddess, the earth mother, and her story is the myth of the maiden, mother and Crone, the triple aspects of generation, preservation and destruction – the cycle of life. It is also a story of letting go and of reconciliation, the archetypal mother and daughter tale.

When we meet Demeter, she is Mother and her Maiden aspect is personified by her daughter, Kore or Persephone. Demeter is one of the many sister-wives of Zeus and she shared the fate of her sisters in that she was swallowed by her father for part of her young life. She is also one of the goddesses who gives birth to a son who becomes her consort, although she is perhaps best known as the archetypal 'one-parent family' in the role of mother of Persephone and it is this aspect on which her myth centres.

Persephone is, naturally enough, a beautiful maiden who is desired by Pluto (Hades), god of the Underworld. He connives with Zeus, the girl's father, to arrange her abduction. One moment Persephone is innocently picking flowers with her companions. The next, as she puts out her hand to a particularly beautiful flower, the earth opens up beneath her feet and Pluto emerges in his chariot, snatches her up and takes her to his kingdom – Hades, the abode of the dead.

Demeter, who had heard Persephone's cries, searches frantically for nine days for her lost daughter. Her grief is so great that she does not eat, sleep or bathe. On the tenth day she meets the third face of woman, the waning-moon goddess Hecate (who has witnessed the abduction but does not impart this information to Demeter). Hecate takes her to Helios, a sun god, who tells Demeter of the plot to kidnap her daughter and who points out Zeus's part in the matter. Helios suggests that she should accept the situation. Demeter, however, refuses to accept the betrayal by her own husband. She retires from Olympus and, disguised as an old woman, wanders the countryside until she is given a job as a nursemaid. Here, she begins to make the child divine. Each night she holds him in a fire to make him immortal. Unfortunately, the child's mother intervenes to stop the process, and Demeter reveals her true identity.

Demeter then causes a temple to be built for her, in which she sits and grieves for her child. This is a serious matter as, being goddess of the corn, without Demeter nothing will grow. Finally, Zeus sends messengers imploring her to return. But, furious still, Demeter refuses until her daughter is returned to her. Hermes, messenger of the gods, is sent to Hades where he, seemingly, finds a depressed and weepy Persephone only too eager to return to her mother. Pluto agrees to return her, but first he gives her pomegranate seeds to eat. When Persephone is reunited with her mother, the first question she is asked is whether she has eaten in the underworld. Had she not accepted the pomegranate seeds,

Persephone could have returned to life above ground permanently. As it is, she has tasted the fruit of knowledge and she must spend part of the year below ground with Pluto as Queen of the Underworld.

After Persephone's return, Demeter gave the Greeks the Eleusinian Mysteries in celebration. These mysteries formed the basis of Greek religion for 2000 years, until the intervention of the Christian priests, although even today traces remain throughout Greece. So secret were the mysteries that no one knows what really happened. The initiates, who were numbered in thousands, swore never to reveal their experiences and, although some of the famous writers who partook in the mysteries have left us hints, no one ever broke that vow. We know that the central theme was renewal and rebirth, and it is believed that the sacred marriage was part of the rites, together with the birth of the divine child, but the rest remains in the collective imagination and can only be accessed through attunement to these goddesses.

The Demeter myth contains many vignettes, one of which is the child who is to be made divine. It is an allegory for the psychological dissolution which splits off the child who is within every woman, who must be purged and purified by fire in order to reveal the goddess within. Unfortunately, most mothers (that is, woman herself) are afraid for the child and refuse to let it go through the ordeal which will bring immortal life. Demeter, as the great mother who has known loss, can facilitate this process of dissolution, purification and reunification with the divine force.

The Demeter archetype

Demeter is the archetypal mother and nurturer; she is the maternal instinct personified and it is the Demeter archetype who suffers from the 'empty nest syndrome' simply because her instinct to have children is so strong and her grief at the loss of her fertility so overwhelming. Her nourishment is not only for her children, however. Demeter provides physical, psychological and spiritual nurturing for all – particularly in the 'helping professions'. Nevertheless, Demeter also encompasses the opposite principle. When the goddess's child is taken away, she rages and cuts off support for mankind. The earth becomes barren.

When the Demeter-woman's 'child' leaves home, she may well fall into deep depression and see this as 'the end', no matter what other responsibilities she may have. Her response to loss or threat is to withhold nurturing; to refuse to meet the needs of others or of herself. So the Demeter-woman's reaction to midlife may well be to withdraw, to be unavailable. For instance, her children who have made lives for themselves may find that they are approved of only if that life fits into what mother knows will be right for them. Her husband may find that he has lost his wife while she struggles to let go of her children, or her desire to have children. Demeter-women often see themselves as victims; they give until literally they have nothing left to give and then deeply resent the calls made on their exhausted energies. Above all else, Demeter needs to learn how to say 'No', to make choices rather than to be compelled to nurture.

The Demeter shadow is possessiveness allied to fear of loss, purposelessness and depression. It is 'passive aggression', hostility that is hidden and fearful, based on unspoken resentment and unacknowledged feelings. It 'forgets to do' rather than saying a clear 'No'. Demeter is afraid of the Underworld (that is the unconscious) and refuses to allow her daughter to go through the psychological integration that exploring the depths of the psyche can bring. The Demeter shadow, therefore, may prefer 'helping' someone, and thereby keeping them dependent, to allowing them to explore their own shadow and become whole once more. It can also be an exploitative shadow, manipulating and manoeuvring to get its own way. This shadow is the mother who has to be nurtured by her children, who must be placated and wooed for fear she turns into the devouring mother: her unspoken threat is loss of love.

The positive Demeter-woman, on the other hand, has faced loss and come through with increased wisdom so she can accompany others on their journey. She has learnt how to mother herself, to be her own child, with love and generosity but also with a protective awareness that allows her to know when enough is enough (both for herself and others). She has an attunement to the cycles of nature; she understands the need for death; how to be in the dark place where new seeds sprout without constantly poking around to be sure they have germinated. She is content to wait for everything to mature in its season, knowing that the harvest will come.

The Persephone archetype

Persephone has two faces. Her 'young' face is the maiden, the Kore, who was an integral part of the fertility trinity. Her much more ancient face is the mature goddess, the Queen of the Underworld who rules over dead souls and who can guide the living who wish to journey there. Interestingly enough, as Jean Bolen points out,[2] none of the Greek heroes who journeyed to meet her ever found her absent, despite the Demeter myth allowing her to spend two-thirds of the year above ground with her mother. Nor is she an innocent, faithful to her husband. In at least one myth, she fights with Aphrodite over the beautiful Adonis (who, ironically, had been sent to her for safe-keeping). This myth is an allegory involving the consort who died and rises again: whilst in Persephone's keeping he is dead, but returned to Aphrodite, goddess of love, he is life itself and the return of fertility.

If a woman is attuned to the Kore archetype, she is ever-youthful, sexually unawakened and uncommitted, often totally dependent on her mother. She frequently acts out the part of 'anima-woman' for men – seemingly all things to all men because, pliable and unformed, she reflects what they wish to see, she who delights in pleasing. Clearly, this characteristic can also form part of the Persephone shadow, and a singular naivety and insularity can lie at the heart of the apparently lustful woman who finds her own unawakened sexuality and lack of commitment reflected back to her in the men who, in her eyes, reject her desire for closeness and union. Such a woman may, either actually or meta-phorically, find herself living the abduction and rape of Persephone when Pluto bursts through from the underworld: potentially as a crisis which activates and moves her into the mature Persephone role, although it may merely be a repetitive pattern.

This 'unawakened' Persephone, powerless and passive, is, in the Woolgers' opinion,[3] the 'eternal, sacrificial victim' projecting all her power 'out there' onto mother, matriarch or man and eternally recreating the conditions which lead to her downfall. Such a maiden desperately needs to be handed over to the dark powers for a journey down into her own unconscious, so that they can be made sacred and incorporated into her being through an initiation of the mature spirit. She is then the reconciliation of the opposites of dark and light, the integration of the powerful, unconscious forces of the psyche with the brightness of consciousness.

When the mature, receptive Persephone archetype is activated, this is the guide to the underworld: the woman who is at home in the realm of the intuition and unconscious, and who has the capacity for deeply moving spiritual and sexual experiences which take her beyond herself to unity with the cosmos. She is psychic and perceptive, tuned to forces beyond the comprehension of most women, and is the potential midwife for birthing the sacred nature in every woman.

The mature Persephone archetype can be very helpful for women who have undergone any kind of abuse. Mature Persephone has regained her power, has overcome her abduction and violation, and has found healing in the darkness. The positive Persephone-woman is at home within the depths of the psyche, and can act as a guide for others journeying into their own unconscious. She is attuned to the birth-death-rebirth cycle and may find herself instinctively drawn to work with the dying, aiding them not only in their transition to another life but also showing them how to live fully until they die.

THE CRONE

HECATE

The myth

Hecate is the ancient goddess of the crossroads, the all-seeing eye who looks in three directions at once; ruling heaven, earth and the underworld. She is a divinity associated with magic and prophecy. Hecate is believed to have evolved from the Egyptian goddess Hekat, a Wise Woman who was in command of 'the Mother's words of power' and who, as a sacred midwife, delivered the sun each morning.

She was originally a goddess reflecting the three phases of the moon, who symbolized the three ages of woman, Maiden, Mother and Crone, but was later said to be a child of Hera and Zeus. In this particular myth, she incurred the wrath of her mother (by stealing Hera's rouge) and hid in the bed of a woman who was giving birth. The contact with the puerperal blood rendered Hecate impure and she was plunged into the Acheron (one of the rivers leading to Hades) to cleanse her, as a result of which she became a goddess of the Underworld.

The goddess of enchantment and magic, she haunted tombs. The victims of murder were often buried at a crossroads, hence her link to the crossroads although the symbolism is much deeper than this and Hecate is linked to choices and to The Way. She is at her most powerful when the Moon wanes, the instinctual time, and she rules the great crossroads of a woman's life, such as puberty, marriage and menopause when this power is closest to the surface. She has a torch to light the darkness and thus performs the function of taking one deep into oneself, and of linking the conscious mind with the unconscious. She is therefore an excellent guide for inner work. She is also a goddess of purification who presides at initiations and rituals.

She witnessed the abduction of Persephone and was able to act as mediator when Demeter tried to rescue her daughter; thus she has the function of bringing together lost parts of the self. Indeed, Hecate can be seen to be presiding over Persephone's initiation and descent into the unconscious, accompanying her return and spiritual illumination. In Hecate we have the completion of the trinity: the Crone is united with Mother and Maiden.

The archetype

The Hecate-woman is the link between the different levels of consciousness and can move between them with confidence. She understands the magical dimension of life. Not afraid to face death and old age, she is unlikely to withhold her power for fear of men – over whom she may well hold a dark enchantment. She is the Morgan la Fey of the Arthurian legends, a woman who fascinates men with her aura of mystique and magic, and the threat of her power.

The Hecate shadow may well be linked to this fascination, and to dark powers used unconsciously to manipulate and coerce those around her. Her link to the depths is great, but her awareness is shallow and therefore everything dark and mysterious is projected onto 'another'. Thus, in the outer world, the Hecate shadow will constantly encounter that which she avoids owning in herself: power. When the Hecate-woman does not consciously own her power, and thereby use it wisely, she may well take others down into the darkness but deny responsibility, ensuring their disintegration.

The positive Hecate archetype is extremely helpful for those making the midlife rite of passage. As Crone, Hecate lights the way and shares her sacred wisdom. She is the third age of woman. When the Hecate-woman consciously integrates her shadow and owns her power, she can act as a light for those who are penetrating their own darkness and can bring together the lost parts of the self.

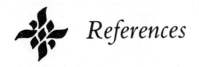

References

INTRODUCTION

1. M. Hunter. *Your Menopause*, Pandora, 1990, p. 159.
2. Ibid, p. xi.
3. A. Mankowitz. *Change of Life*, Inner City Books, 1984.
4. M. Sjoo & B. Mor. *The Great Cosmic Mother*, Harper & Row, 1987.
5. P. Weideger. *Menstruation and Menopause*, Dell Publications Inc., New York, 1977.
6. Source unknown. (This was given to me by a course tutor who had been given it by the author but did not know her name.)
7. Information in this section is taken, amongst other sources, from *Menstruation and Menopause* (as above) and *The Curse*, J. Delaney, M. Care Lipton & E. Toth, E. P. Dutton Inc., New York, 1976.
8. Teresa Gorman, MP, and Dr Malcolm Whitehead. *The Amarant Book of Hormone Replacement Therapy*, Pan, 1989.
9. Ibid.
10. *The Great Cosmic Mother*.
11. R. M. Rilke. *Letter to a Young Poet*.
12. A. Richardson. *Earth God Rising*, Llewellyn, 1990.
13. *The Great Cosmic Mother*, p 193.
14. Quoted in *Kali, The Feminine Force*, A. Mookerjee. Thames and Hudson, 1988, p. 6.

CHAPTER 1

1. J. Lyttleton. 'Topics in Gynaecology – Menopause', *Journal of Chinese Medicine*, 33.
2. H. L. Jones. A. C. Wentz & L. S. Burnett, *Novak's Textbook of Gynecology* (11th Edition), Williams & Wilkins, 1988.
3. M. M. Shargold. 'Exercise in the post menopausal woman'. *Obstet Gynecol.*, 75: pp. 535–85, 1990.
4. J. Lyttleton, 'Topics in menopause – osteoporosis'. *Journal of Chinese Medicine*, 34; pp. 5–11, 1990.

5. T. Garrett & J. Studd. 'What age to stop HRT?' *Update*, Jan 1990; pp. 115–23.

CHAPTER 2

1. H. Lee Wolfe. *Second Spring: A guide to healthy menopause through traditional Chinese medicine*, p. 45, Blue Poppy Press, 1990.
2. M. Grieve. *A Modern Herbal*, Jonathan Cape Ltd, 1985, and H. A. Guerber. *Myths and Legends. Greece and Rome*, Studio Editions, 1986.
3. M. Stuart (ed). *The Encylopaedia of Herbs and Herbalism*, Macdonald & Co., 1987.
4. J. Benveniste. *Nature*, June 1989; pp. 816–88.
5. *British Medical Journal*, 6772; pp. 316–23, 1991.
6. *Journal of Complementary Medicine*, Feb 1986.
7. *Second Spring*, p. 27.
8. I. Veith (trans). *The Yellow Emperor's Classic of Internal Medicine*, University of California Press, Berkeley, 1966.
9. R. O. Becker. 'The role of electric potential at the cellular level in growth and development.' *Ann NY Acad Sci*, 238; pp. 451–6, 1974.
10. J. N. Kenyon, MD. *21st Century Medicine*, Thorsons, 1986.
11. J. N. Kenyon, MD. *Modern Techniques of Acupuncture, Vol. III*, Thorsons, 1985.

CHAPTER 3

1. *Menstruation and Menopause*, p. 228.
2. P. Shuttleworth and P. Redgrave. *The Wise Wound*, Paladin, 1978.

CHAPTER 4

1. *Your Menopause*, p. 31.
2. *The Wise Wound*.
3. E. Kubler-Ross. *Death: The Final Stage of Growth*, Spectrum, 1975.
4. P. Krystal. *Cutting the Ties that Bind*, Element Books, 1990.

CHAPTER 5

1.   B. Hand Clow, *Chiron: The Rainbow Bridge*, p. 201, Llewellyn, 1990.
2.   T. Dethlefsen and R. Dahlke. *The Healing Power of Illness*, Element Books, 1990.
3.   *Your Menopause.*
4.   A. Dickson. *The Mirror Within*, Quartet, 1985.
5.   Ibid., pp. 59, 60.
6.   M. Chia and M. Chia. *Healing Love through the Tao: cultivating female sexual energy*, Healing Tao Books, New York, 1986.
7.   E. Bass and L. Davis. *The Courage to Heal: A guide for women survivors of child sexual abuse*, Cedar, USA, 1988.

CHAPTER 6

1.   J. Shinoda Bolen. *Goddesses in Everywoman*, p. 6, Harper & Row, 1984.
2.   *Goddesses in Everywoman*, as above, and J. B. Woolger and R. J. Woolger, *The Goddess Within*, Rider, 1990.
3.   N. Hall. *The Moon and The Virgin*, Women's Press, 1980.
4.   E. C. Whitmont. *Return of the Goddess*, p. 203, Arkana, 1983.
5.   B. Black Koltuv. *The Book of Lilith*, Nicolas-Hayes Inc., York Beach, USA, 1986.
6.   P. Redgrove. *The Black Goddess and the Sixth Sense*, p. 186, Paladin, 1989.
7.   B. Walker. *The Crone*, Harper Collins, 1988.
8.   Information in this section has been taken largely from B. Walker, *The Women's Encyclopaedia of Myths and Secrets*, Harper & Row, 1983.
9.   Quoted in N. Douglas & P. Slinger, *Sexual Secrets*, p. 355, Destiny Books, New York, 1979.
10.   Ibid., p. 354.
11.   *The Black Goddess*, p. 186.
12.   R. Masters. *The Goddess Sekhmet*, Amity House, New York, 1988.
13.   *Earth God Rising.*

CHAPTER 7

1. *Return of the Goddess*, p. 197.
2. J. K. Brown, *et al. In Her Prime*, Bergin & Garvey Publishers Inc., Massachusetts, 1985.
3. *Menstruation and Menopause*, p. 227.
4. *In Her Prime*, p. 23.
5. Ibid, p. 146.
6. T. King O'Brien (ed.). *The Spiral Path*, Yes International Publishers, St Paul, USA, 1988.
7. Ibid, pp. ix, 67.
8. E. Begg. *The Cult of the Black Virgin*, Arkana, 1985.
9. A. Howell. *Jungian Synchronicity*, Quest Books, 1990.
10. *The Crone*, p. 31.
11. *In Her Prime*, p. 87.
12. L. B. Rubin. *Women of a Certain Age*, p. 68, Harper Collins, 1981.
13. D. Boater. Article in *Metamorphosis*, Autumn 1984.
14. B. Edwards. *Drawing on the Right Side of the Brain*, Fontana, 1982.
15. Tape available from Matthew Manning Centre, Buryfields, Cage End, Hatfield Broad Oak, Herts CM22 7HT.
16. M. Freely. 'We Shall Not Be Moved', *The Independent on Sunday*, 14 July 1991.
17. *The Moon and the Virgin*.
18. *Second Spring*, p. 154.
19. Moontime (tape). Brooke Medicine Eagle.

CONCLUSION

1. *In Her Prime*, p. 206.
2. 'Woman', © Julie Felix 1990.

APPENDIX II

1. *The Moon and the Virgin*, p. 240.
2. *Goddesses in Everywoman*.
3. *The Goddess Within*, p. 247.

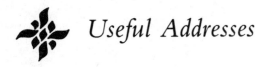 # Useful Addresses

Dr Robert Jacobs and Judy Hall (sae please)
c/o Element Books
The Courtyard
Bell Street
Shaftesbury
Dorset SP7 8BP

COUNSELLING

Practitioners' list:

British Association for Counselling
37a Sheep Street
Rugby
Warks CV21 3BX

INFORMATION ON HRT

Amarant Trust
80 Lambeth Road
London SE1

WESTERN HERBALISM

Practitioners' list:

National Institute of Medical Herbalists
41 Hatherley Road
Winchester
Hants SO22 6RR

Suppliers:

East West Herbs Ltd.
Langston Priory Mews
Kingham
Oxfordshire OX7 6UP

HOMOEOPATHY

Practitioners' list:

British Homoeopathic Association
27a Devonshire Street
London WC1N 1RJ

Suppliers:

Ainsworths Homoeopathic Pharmacy
38 New Cavendish Street
London W1M 7LH

Weleda (UK) Ltd.
Heanor Road
Ilkeston
Derbyshire DE7 8DR

COMPLEX HOMOEOPATHY

Practitioners' list:

Noma (Complex Homoeopathy Ltd)
Unit 3
1–16 Hollybrook Road
Off Winchester Road
Upper Shirley
Southampton SO1 6RB
(also supplies remedies to qualified practitioners)

CHINESE MEDICINE

Practitioners' lists:

British Medical Acupuncture Society
Newton House
Newton Lane
Lower Whitley
Warrington
Cheshire WA4 4JA

International College of Oriental Medicine
Green Hedges House
Green Hedges Avenue
East Grinstead
Sussex RH19 1DZ

Register of Chinese Herbal Medicine
c/o Midsummer Cottage Clinic
Nether Westcote
Kingham
Oxfordshire OX7 6SD

Suppliers (herbs and electro-stimulators):

Acumedic Centre
101–103 Camden High Street
London NW1 7JN

East West Herbs Ltd
(see above)

Mayway (UK) Ltd
34 Greek Street
London W1

Mayway Trading Corp.
780 Broadway
San Francisco
USA 94133

 *Index*